HISTORY OF
THE ANCIENT AND MEDIEVAL WORLD

SECOND EDITION

VOLUME 2

WESTERN ASIA AND THE MEDITERRANEAN

mc **Marshall Cavendish**
Reference
New York

Marshall Cavendish
99 White Plains Road
Tarrytown, New York 10591

www.marshallcavendish.us

Library of Congress Cataloging-in-Publication Data

History of the ancient and medieval world / [edited by Henk Dijkstra]. -- 2nd ed.
    v. cm.
 Includes bibliographical references and index.
 Contents: v. 1. The first civilizations -- v. 2. Western Asia and the Mediterranean -- v. 3. Ancient Greece -- v. 4. The Roman Empire -- v. 5. The changing shape of Europe -- v. 6. The early Middle Ages in western Asia and Europe -- v. 7. Southern and eastern Asia -- v. 8. Europe in the Middle Ages -- v. 9. Western Asia, northern Europe, and Africa in the Middle Ages -- v. 10. The passing of the medieval world -- v. 11. Index.
 ISBN 978-0-7614-7789-1 (set) -- ISBN 978-0-7614-7791-4 (v. 1) -- ISBN 978-0-7614-7792-1 (v. 2) -- ISBN 978-0-7614-7793-8 (v. 3) -- ISBN 978-0-7614-7794-5 (v. 4) -- ISBN 978-0-7614-7795-2 (v. 5) -- ISBN 978-0-7614-7796-9 (v. 6) -- ISBN 978-0-7614-7797-6 (v. 7) -- ISBN 978-0-7614-7798-3 (v. 8) -- ISBN 978-0-7614-7799-0 (v. 9) -- ISBN 978-0-7614-7800-3 (v. 10) -- ISBN 978-0-7614-7801-0 (v. 11)
 1. History, Ancient. 2. Middle Ages. 3. Civilization, Medieval. I. Dijkstra, Henk.
 D117.H57 2009
 940.1--dc22

                    2008060052

Printed in Malaysia

12 11 10 09 08 7 6 5 4 3 2 1

General Editor: Henk Dijkstra

Marshall Cavendish
Project Editor: Brian Kinsey
Publisher: Paul Bernabeo
Production Manager: Michael Esposito

Brown Reference Group
Project Editor: Chris King
Text Editors: Shona Grimbly, Charles Phillips
Designer: Lynne Lennon
Cartographers: Joan Curtis, Darren Awuah
Picture Researcher: Laila Torsun
Indexer: Christine Michaud
Managing Editor: Tim Cooke

PICTURE CREDITS

SET CONTENTS

VOLUME CONTENTS

THE HITTITES

In the second millennium BCE, a tribe of formidable warriors based in Anatolia (present-day Turkey) built an empire that was to rival those of ancient Babylon and Egypt and last for 500 years. They were known as the Hittites.

The Hittites were a group of Indo-European peoples who migrated from central Asia some time around 2000 BCE. They conquered an area of Anatolia called Hatti, from which they got their name. The region was to become the center of a vast empire that stretched deep into Syria to the south. The Hittites flourished from around 1700 to 1200 BCE and were one of the major powers of western Asia.

In Assyrian and Egyptian sculptures, the Hittites are portrayed as powerful-looking men with flat foreheads, slanted eyes, and hair in braids hanging down their backs. They vaguely resemble later Turks and Mongols. However, in other sculptures, the Hittites are pictured with different features, leading some historians to conclude that they came from a mixture of races.

Hattushash

The center of the Hittites' domain was the mountainous central region of Anatolia, and their capital was the great city of Hattushash (see box, page 154), set in a natural fortress position in the north of this region. The history of the Hittites begins around 1850 BCE, when a prince called Anittas set out to extend his small kingdom in central Anatolia by conquering the cities of Kanesh and Hattushash. Although Hattushash was located in a commanding position, Anittas destroyed it completely and declared its ground to be cursed. Several generations later, another king, called Labarnas, decided to rebuild Hattushash and make it his capital. To commemorate the event, Labarnas changed his name to Hattusilis (meaning "man of Hattushash").

It was this king, Hattusilis I (ruled c. 1650–1620 BCE), who was the real founder of the Hittite Empire. He was eager to conquer new territory, and after consolidating his position in central Anatolia he marched his army south across the Taurus Mountains to the Mediterranean Sea. Turning east, he invaded northern Syria, a region that was then ruled by the kings of a city called Aleppo. From Syria, Hattusilis brought back a band of scribes, whose task was to teach cuneiform writing to the Hittites.

Hattusilis was succeeded by his grandson, Mursilis I, who was equally imperialist in his mind-set. First, Mursilis conquered Aleppo. Then, marching east along the Euphrates River, he invaded Mesopotamia, sacking Babylon in 1595 BCE. However, while the Hittite army was returning home, it was attacked by the Hurrians, an aggressive tribe based

This sculpture depicts a Hittite god. In art, Hittite gods were often shown wearing horned helmets.

on the upper Euphrates River. The Hittite army was routed, and when Mursilis finally managed to reach home, he was murdered by his brother-in-law. While conflicts within the royal family escalated, this first Hittite Empire went into rapid decline.

This statue depicts Tarunza, a Hittite king who ruled the city of Malatya.

The New Kingdom

The next major chapter in Hittite history began in the early 14th century BCE, when King Suppiluliumas I (ruled c. 1358–1323 BCE) founded the New Kingdom. Suppiluliumas dedicated himself to restoring the fortunes of the Hittites and began by reconquering the territories in southern Anatolia that had previously been Hittite possessions. He then advanced into Syria, where he conquered several city-states, reaching as far south as Damascus. Turning east, Suppiluliumas sought to subdue the Hurrians and defeated them at the Battle of Carchemish. He then turned the Hurrians' kingdom into a vassal state by installing a minor Hurrian prince on the throne, making him swear loyalty to the Hittites, and marrying him to a Hittite princess.

Suppiluliumas also turned the conquered Syrian cities into vassals. By doing so, he built up an empire of confederate states that owed allegiance to the Hittites. They were bound by treaty to pay a substantial annual tribute to their masters. At the same time, they supplied a number of soldiers to the Hittite army. Suppiluliumas's success in expanding his empire depended both on the efficient organization of his new Hittite state, which was run along strictly military lines, and on his extremely formidable army (see box, page 157).

Suppiluliumas's successors were equally dedicated to maintaining and expanding the Hittite Empire. They waged war against neighboring tribes and took on the might of Egypt, which was trying to halt the Hittite expansion. Suppiluliumas's son, Mursilis II, fought the mountain tribes to the north and succeeded in extending Hittite domination westward to the Aegean coast. There he created a series of vassal states. To protect his kingdom from attacks from the north, Mursilis built a line of

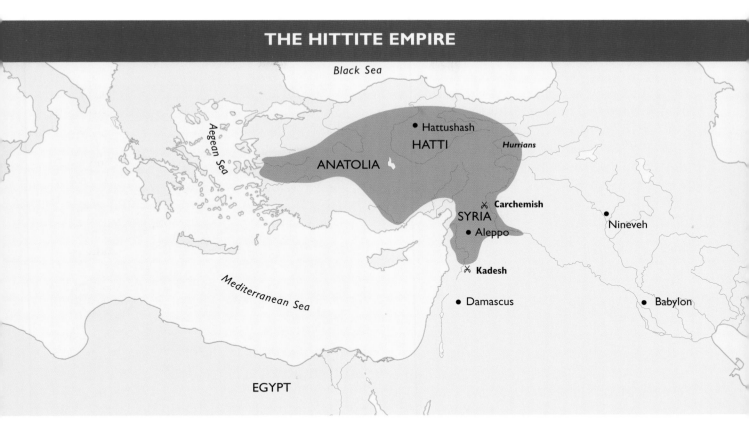

THE HITTITE EMPIRE

fortresses that were permanently garrisoned by soldiers.

Despite Mursilis's efforts, the kingdom came under renewed attack from northern tribes during the reign of his successor, Muwatallis. The end result of these attacks was the destruction of Hattushash. In response, Muwatallis moved his capital city farther south. He also subdued the vassal states of Arzawa in the west, which were in revolt.

The Battle of Kadesh

Having resecured the loyalty of the Arzawa states, Muwatallis went to war with Egypt, which was then under the rule the Pharaoh Ramses II. Ramses was anxious to retake the Hittite cities in Syria that had formerly been under Egyptian control. In 1275 BCE, Muwatallis assembled an enormous army and lay in wait for the Egyptians behind the city of Kadesh. As the Egyptians entered the city from the south, the Hittite army took

them by surprise. What followed was one of the greatest battles of ancient history, which is said to have involved around 5,000 chariots. Initially, the Hittites had the upper hand, but the late arrival of reinforcements helped the Egyptians drive their enemies back. Ramses claimed victory, but it seems more likely that the battle ended in a stalemate. In any case, the Hittites remained in control of Syria.

Hattusilis III (ruled c. 1275–1250 BCE) concluded peace treaties with both Egypt and Babylon. The treaty with Egypt was sealed by the marriage of a Hittite princess to Ramses. For a time, the Hittite Empire enjoyed an unparalleled period of peace and prosperity, but in the second half of the 13th century, it was threatened by the growing power of the Assyrian Empire to the east. In the west, meanwhile, warrior races known as the Sea Peoples were threatening the coast of Anatolia. It is thought that the

KEY

Extent of Hittite Empire in 1400 BCE

⚔ Major battle

HATTUSHASH

Hattushash, the capital of the Hittite Empire, was founded by King Hattusilis I around 1650 BCE. Its ruins lie in central Turkey, close to a present-day village called Bogazkoy. Hattushash was built on a high, rocky ridge, making it a natural fortress. Because much of the ground was sloping, earth terraces were constructed to provide flat ground on which to build houses.

The city covered an area of around 400 acres (162 ha) and was encircled by a massive rampart 4 miles (6 km) long. This encircling fortification consisted of a great earthen embankment surmounted by a stone wall with towers and battlements. The gates that led into the city were decorated with large relief sculptures carved into stone—twin sphinxes at the Sphinx Gate, two ferocious lions at the Lion Gate, and a young soldier complete with battle-ax at the King's Gate.

The city was carefully planned, with streets as straight as the land allowed. A drainage channel ran down the center of the bigger streets, covered over with large slabs of stone. This channel received dirty water from the houses on either side, through a system of smaller pipes.

The houses in Hattushash were constructed on stone foundations, with walls of sun-dried mud bricks. Flat roofs made of mud and brushwood were laid over wooden beams. There were few windows, so the houses were very dark inside. The floors were made of either flagstone or beaten earth, and most houses had a hearth for a fire and an oven. Some houses had a stone sink connected to the drain, and clay baths have also been found. There was little furniture, so most people ate their meals and slept on the floor.

In the Lower Town (in the northern part of the city), there was a great temple set in an enormous enclosure, roughly square shaped,

The ruins of the Hittite capital at Hattushash. The city was the center of the Hittite Empire from around 1650 to 1190 BCE.

measuring about 900 feet (275 m) on each side. This area was surrounded by a precinct wall that in part coincided with the wall of the lower city. On the eastern side of the city, towering over the Lower Town, stood the citadel, on which was built a magnificent palace with pillared walkways for the king. Although all the buildings have long been destroyed, it is thought that the palace contained several courtyards, around which were grouped the royal residences and a large audience hall.

At its height, Hattushash was a bustling city, the center of a great empire. It would have been an important market place for local farmers and for traveling merchants selling their wares. The city contained many taverns, eating houses, granaries, and craftsmen's workshops, and the streets would have been thronged with thousands of people going about their business.

Sea Peoples probably overran Anatolia around 1190 BCE, sacking Hattushash (once again the capital city) and destroying the Hittite Empire.

The Neo-Hittites

In Syria, the cities that had been conquered by the Hittites retained a Hittite identity for the following five centuries. In this so-called Neo-Hittite kingdom, the most important town was Carchemish. Situated alongside one of the three fords across the Euphrates River, Carchemish was well placed to dominate the major trade route from Nineveh to the Mediterranean Sea. Carchemish was also almost impregnable. Although it was often attacked, the town remained unconquered until it succumbed to the Assyrian king Sargon II in 717 BCE.

Hittite society

The king was at the top of Hittite society, combining the roles of military commander, supreme ruler, chief priest, and highest judge. He was supported by nobles and officials who were generally members of his own family. In order to secure the loyalty of the cities and provinces throughout the empire, the king would usually put the local governments in the hands of his family members or arrange a royal marriage to achieve the same ends.

The society was feudal, meaning that the nobles and provincial vassals each had to swear a personal oath of loyalty to the king. In return, the nobles held large tracts of land, each with its own retainers, such as peasants and artisans, who in turn had to swear loyalty to their lord. The

This relief sculpture found at Yazilikaya depicts a procession of Hittite gods and goddesses. Yazilikaya was a religious sanctuary located near Hattushash.

retainers also had to pay annual dues, either in goods or services, such as working on the lord's land or doing military service.

Most of the Hittite people were peasant farmers who worked on the land, growing wheat and barley, along with peas and onions. They also cultivated apple, fig, and olive trees, as well as grape vines. Wool, meat, and milk were provided by herds of sheep, pigs, and cattle.

Crafts

Skilled artisans and craftspeople made up an important section of Hittite society. There were stonemasons, carpenters, potters, and metalsmiths. Doctors, tailors, cobblers, bakers, merchants, and innkeepers could also be found in the cities.

Hittite metalworkers were highly skilled in both bronze working and, from around 1700 BCE, the technique of iron smelting. In most parts of the world, the Iron Age had not yet begun and the pioneering art of smelting was a closely guarded secret. Local mines provided ingots of raw iron ore, which were transported to refineries where they were

This sanctuary at Eflatun Pinar was a place of worship during the time of the Hittite Empire.

heated to high temperatures to extract iron. Iron was used to make tools and weapons, but because it was scarce, most weapons were still made of bronze. Silver, used as a medium of exchange, was mined in the Taurus Mountains, where there was an abundance of the metal.

The Hittites wore woolen clothes, woven from yarn spun at home. Men wore a long-sleeve, knee-length tunic, usually belted at the waist and fastened with bronze pins at the shoulders. Another longer tunic, known as a Hurrian shirt, was reserved for special occasions such as festivals and was embroidered or decorated with bronze ornaments. Women wore lighter clothes, with a long woolen cloak for outdoors. Both men and women wore their hair long, sometimes in a pigtail, and both sexes wore jewelry such as necklaces, bracelets, rings, and earrings.

Hittite art

The most important period of Hittite artistic development lasted from 1450 to 1200 BCE and drew on earlier sources

THE HITTITE ARMY

To achieve their imperialistic aims, the Hittite kings needed an efficient fighting force. A small permanent troop of infantry served as the king's bodyguard and also carried out other duties such as patrolling the empire's frontiers. However, when the king embarked on a military campaign, a much larger force, numbering up to 30,000 men, was needed.

The soldiers were recruited from the estates of the Hittite nobles or from satellite kingdoms. Sometimes their numbers were augmented by mercenaries. The army consisted of two main divisions—foot soldiers and charioteers. The charioteers were highly skilled. The horse-drawn

chariots were built of timber and were lightweight, fast, and exceptionally maneuverable. However, the chariots were also easily overturned, so a steady nerve and a sure hand were needed to keep them upright in a charge. Each chariot carried three men—a charioteer to drive the chariot, a warrior with a spear, and a soldier with a shield to protect the other two.

Following behind the chariots came the infantry, which were armed with daggers, long spears, and sickle-shaped swords that were used with a slashing movement. Some soldiers also used axes and bows and arrows. For protection in battle, the soldiers wore pointed helmets, with hanging flaps that covered the cheeks and neck. Sometimes, the foot soldiers wore body armor made of small overlapping scales of bronze, covered by a leather tunic, and carried shields to ward off blows.

As supreme military commander, the king generally led his army into battle himself. Lesser commands were held by members of the nobility. The army was divided into units of 10, 100, and 1,000 men. All units were subjected to rigorous training that resulted in a highly disciplined and efficient fighting force, which meant that troops could be moved quickly and secretly into position to make a surprise attack.

It is not known how the soldiers were paid. A large army was expensive to maintain, and it is probable that the troops lived by plundering the local inhabitants when in enemy territory. After a success in battle, booty was distributed liberally, which gave the army an extra incentive to be on the victorious side.

This statue depicts a Hittite soldier, wearing the pointed helmet that was typically used by Hittite troops at the time of the empire.

from Sumer and Babylon, as well as local Anatolian influences from the third millennium BCE. Hittite metalworkers produced elaborate bronze and gold ornaments, while Hittite potters produced jugs, cups, and vases, sometimes modeled in the shape of animals or birds. The Hittites were skilled at carving. Some particularly impressive representations of their deities were found at Carchemish. Made to adorn a royal robe, these ornaments were carved in lapis lazuli and mounted on gold.

Stonemasons made giant stone relief sculptures of animals, humans, and gods. In one great sanctuary, a magnificent series of mythological scenes, discovered carved

in rock, depicts lions and sphinxes serving gods and goddesses. Other carvings have shown gods wearing high pointed hats, short-skirted robes, and boots with long curling toes, clothes that identify them as part of the pantheon of Mesopotamian and northern Syrian gods adopted by the Hittites.

Reliefs at Carchemish suggest that music and dancing were popular with the later Hittites. One relief depicts soldiers

This gravestone depicts a Hittite nobleman and his wife from Marash, which was an important Hittite city.

VILLAGE LIFE

Most people in Hittite society did not live in a town or city but in small village communities that were largely self-sufficient. Each village had its own area of agricultural land, which was separated from the land of other nearby villages by tracts of fallow land. The villagers grew their crops and pastured their animals on the land belonging to their village, most of which was held in common.

Some of the inhabitants of a village might not be native Hittites but people who had been relocated from conquered regions. These new arrivals were settled on Hittite land and helped to increase the productivity of the village. There would also be some craftsmen living in the village, and they might hold individual plots of land on lease. In addition to their services as crafts-

men, they were required to spend time working on community projects such as digging irrigation channels and sinking wells.

Village life was governed by a body of senior members of the community, or elders. The elders were responsible for maintaining law and order in the village and for protecting any strangers who arrived on village land. An elder was usually the head of a household and as such had the power to give his daughters away in marriage.

As well as producing enough food to feed themselves, the villagers had to pay regular taxes to the central government. Native-born Hittite citizens also had to serve a term of military duty when required.

dancing, wearing animal skins and hiding their faces behind masks. Other reliefs show more scenes from day-to-day life, such as the king speaking to his vizier, with his hand resting on the vizier's shoulder, and a queen carrying a small prince on her arm, with the prince leading a tame ox by a rope.

Religion

The Hittites originally tended to worship a local god, and their prayers were primarily directed at securing favorable weather to ensure a good harvest. As the empire became unified, a centralized form of religion developed, incorporating a large number of deities. As chief priest, it became the duty of the king to travel around the country and preside over important religious festivals. It was believed that if a king neglected this duty, perhaps because he was away on a military campaign, the gods would become angry and the state would suffer. Mursilis II was noted for his pious observance of his priestly duties, and several of his prayers have survived. In one prayer, he begged the gods to intercede to save people from a dreadful plague that was ravaging the nation.

Archives found at Hattushash give many details about the large pantheon of deities worshipped in the Old Hittite period, together with descriptions of the ceremonies and hymns of the various religious cults. Texts relating ancient myths also clarify the complex nature of the cults, some of which seem to have been derived and adapted from other cultures. A common theme in many of the myths is one of order and chaos, and the related battles of the gods.

Many myths of the Old Hittite period feature storm gods and sun deities.

Some myths appear to have been derived from older traditional Hatti ones. One story tells of a battle between a storm god and the serpent monster Illuyanka. In the later empire period, other myths were adopted from the conquered Hurrians. Some stories involved Teshup, the storm god, who was to become the head of the Hittite pantheon of deities. Teshup was often accompanied by his consort Arinna, the sun goddess. A powerful rival of Teshup was Kumarbi, the god of grain and the harvest. Some deities were also adopted from the Mesopotamian and Syrian religions, including Ishtar, the goddess of war, who was called Shauska by the Hittites.

Lions were popular subjects for Hittite sculptors. This is one of several surviving statues of the animal.

159

THE DISAPPEARING GOD

Among the many myths that told stories of the gods of the Hittites was the one of the disappearing god. This story had several versions, but in all of them a god withdraws from the world, either in a fit of anger or because he wants to indulge himself in a pleasurable pursuit, such as hunting.

In one version, Telepinu, the god of fertility and agriculture, became annoyed with the world, lost his temper, and vanished. In doing so, he caused all life on earth to shrivel up and die. In another version, it was the sun god that disappeared, leaving the world to succumb to cold and frost. In all versions of the story, the other gods frantically search without success for the god that is missing. One account tells how the goddess Hannahanna (meaning "grandmother") has the idea of sending a bee to find the god. The bee has no difficulty in locating the god, and once it has found him, it stings him. The bee then puts wax over the sting to stop the pain and guides the errant god back to the others. When the disappearing god has returned, the world begins to thrive once more.

Nature deities, particularly those of mountains, rivers, and springs, were worshipped by the Hittites.

One of the most important religious sites for the Hittites was the ravine sanctuary at Yazilikaya. A relief carved in rock at the sanctuary shows a procession of 70 gods and goddesses, some of which are standing on the backs of animals sacred to them. The procession is led by Teshup. In the reliefs, many of the storm gods look very similar. They are shown wearing short kilts with wide belts and tall helmets with horns, and they are holding swords and battle-axes. In their priestly role, kings are shown dressed in caps and long robes and holding a long curved staff, the symbol of a priest. The king is sometimes shown standing before a sacrificial altar and at other times being embraced by a god.

This Hittite altar dates to around 1450 BCE.

Language and writing

It is thought that the Hittites spoke an Indo-European language, probably brought to Anatolia by waves of Indo-European settlers toward the end of the third millennium BCE. The Indo-European languages were derived from Sanskrit, an ancient Indian language, and were to become the basis of Greek and Latin, giving rise to all the modern European languages. Several ancient Hittite words bear a remarkable resemblance to their present-day English equivalents. For example, the Hittite word for "daughter" was *dohter*, while "water" was *watar*.

The Hittites used two writing systems—hieroglyphs (picture writing) and the wedge-shaped signs of the cuneiform script. The hieroglyphic script consisted of signs representing certain ideas, such as king, city, and god, together with other signs representing sounds. The lines of script were read

Cuneiform tablets such as this were used to keep records of transactions as well as to record history. Thousands of Hittite tablets have been found.

alternately from right to left and from left to right, in the same way that a plow makes furrows in the earth.

When the city of Hattushash was excavated in the early 20th century CE, around 20,000 clay tablets of cuneiform writing were found. Historians believe the tablets, which were written in both Akkadian (the international language of diplomacy at the time) and Hittite itself, make up the royal archives. In the years immediately following the tablets' discovery, the Czech scholar Bedrich Hrozny succeeded in deciphering the cuneiform texts, making the Hittite language accessible to modern scholars. He also revealed a history of the Hittite civilization that had been lost for more than 3,000 years.

See also:

The Assyrians (volume 2, page 208) • Egypt's Middle Kingdom (volume 1, page 78)

THE HITTITE LEGAL CODE

A collection of around 200 laws found at Hattushash has provided a remarkable insight into the Hittite legal code. The laws were inscribed on tablets probably around 1500 BCE. The code was one of the most lenient codes of antiquity, being based on restitution rather than retribution. Whereas most other societies used death or mutilation to punish wrongdoing, the Hittites moved toward more humane types of punishment.

Early statutes recorded on the tablets did indeed prescribe death—by drawing and quartering—for a range of crimes including rape and, for slaves, disobedience and black magic. In the case of other crimes, the offender's nose and ears might be cut off. A murder committed outside the city attracted a more severe punishment than one committed inside the city walls—because, it was said, in the countryside there was less chance of the victim's cries for help being heard. However, despite these early harsh punishments, it soon became possible for convicted criminals to substitute an animal to receive the penalty on their behalf, and for murder or theft, the criminals could pay an amount of money in compensation.

The code also provides information about Hittite marriage customs. At a wedding among aristocratic landowners, the husband would give his bride a large dowry, which was kept by the bride's parents. If the couple later divorced, the dowry had to be returned to the husband. If the husband died, his brother had to marry the widow, even if he already had a wife.

BRONZE AGE GREECE

In the third millennium BCE, a relatively sophisticated culture grew up on both the Greek mainland and the surrounding islands. In particular, the inhabitants of the Cyclades began to produce beautiful works of sculpture.

Greece consists of mainland Greece on the Balkan Peninsula and a mass of islands, large and small, scattered over the Aegean Sea and extending as far south as Crete in the Mediterranean. The climate is volatile, with extreme fluctuations in temperature, strong winds, and sudden downpours of torrential rain. The main agricultural products are olives, grapes, and figs. In ancient times, both cattle and horses were grazed in the eastern central regions of mainland Greece.

Greece in the Stone Age

There is evidence of Stone Age hunters living in mainland Greece in the Paleolithic Age, and by the seventh millennium BCE it seems that farming communities were established. These early farmers lived in villages of circular mud huts, grew grains, peas, and lentils, and kept animals, such as pigs, cattle, goats, and sheep, for meat and milk. The farmers supplemented their diet by hunting and fishing and made stone tools such as axes and chisels. By the end of the Neolithic Age, people were living in walled towns, in which some large houses had a central hall—indicating that some individuals had now become wealthier than others, or had even become chieftains.

On the mainland, metalworking invaders arrived in the first part of the third millennium BCE. In addition to a knowledge of bronze, the invaders introduced the swing-plow, which greatly improved farming methods. The period between around 2800 and 2600 BCE (called Early Helladic I) was a time of great change. Walled hilltop villages appeared, with a chief who ruled over the surrounding farmland. Trading with other communities, some of them overseas, led to the emergence of a wealthy class, who built their houses of stone rather than mud bricks. Along with the rise of this merchant class came the craftsman class and the use of symbols to mark goods and seal containers.

During the period called Early Helladic II (c. 2600–2100 BCE), this civilization peaked, building settlements surrounded by towering stone walls and containing houses with several rooms. Excavations at Lerna have uncovered what was probably an important civic building, the massive House of Tiles, which was built two stories high with a balcony on the upper story. The house takes its modern name from a number of small, flat tiles of baked clay that were found in its ruins. The tiles may have covered a sloping roof and are thought to be the earliest roof tiles ever discovered.

From 2100 BCE onward, successive waves of hostile migrants from central Asia swept through the Balkan Peninsula

and destroyed most of the fortified towns. In their place, the invaders built dwellings of more primitive, one-storied, houses. The invaders brought with them a new kind of pottery, which was made on a wheel and whose angular shapes seemed to imitate metal pots. This pottery was first discovered by the German archaeologist Heinrich Schliemann, who uncovered it in the late 19th century CE when he was excavating at Orchomenus, a city in Boeotia that rose to prominence in the Mycenaean era. Schliemann named both the pots and the people who had produced them Minyan. These Minyans spoke an Indo-European language and have since come to be considered the first Greeks.

This marble sculpture, made on the island of Keros around 2000 BCE, depicts a musician playing the harp.

163

This gold goblet dates to around 2100 BCE, an era known to archaeologists as the Early Helladic II period.

The invaders eventually integrated with the indigenous inhabitants and learned from them seafaring skills that had been notably lacking. The general level of culture remained low, however, for the Minyans. They lived in simple "long houses" arranged in villages, and some of the villages were enclosed within walls.

Island cultures

Prior to the Early Helladic I period on the Greek mainland, another culture had started to develop on the Cycladic islands. Located in the southwestern Aegean Sea, the Cyclades are a group of more than 30 major islands formed from the peaks of mountain ranges submerged long ago. The islands are rocky and volcanic and are rich in minerals such as gold, silver, obsidian, and marble, as well as the ores of lead, iron, and copper.

The Cyclades get their name from the Greek word *kyklos*, meaning "circle," because they are arranged roughly in a circle around the island of Delos, which was considered sacred to the god Apollo (see box, page 167). The islands have been inhabited since very early times. There is evidence of settlements on the larger islands, such as Kythnos, Mykonos, Naxos, and Milos, dating from the sixth millennium BCE.

These early Neolithic settlers probably came from southwestern Anatolia (present-day Turkey), and as they were seafaring people, they settled near the coasts on the chosen islands. The settlers grew barley and wheat, raised pigs, sheep,

GREECE IN THE BRONZE AGE

and goats, and caught fish, particularly tuna, in the Aegean. There is evidence from some excavated sites that these people were familiar with copperworking from around 4000 BCE.

Cycladic art

From around 3000 BCE, the Cycladic islanders began to develop a distinct culture of their own. They became expert at carving small, elegant figurines in the pure white marble that they found on the islands of Paros and Naxos. Archaeologists have discovered these statuettes in burial chambers. To achieve a smooth surface, the figures were rubbed with emery stones, a dark, very hard rock that the sculptors obtained from Naxos. Details were then often picked out in red and blue paint.

The figurines are extremely distinctive in their style. To begin with, they almost always portray women rather than men. The elongated figures stand upright with the head tilted back, while the arms are usually folded across the chest, with the left arm above the right. The legs and feet touch one another. The statues vary in size enormously; the smallest are only 2 inches (5 cm) tall, while the largest are almost life-size.

Archaeologists are unsure about the purpose of these statuettes. Because many of these figurines were found in

The early inhabitants of Greece were skilled at metalworking. This gold headband from around 2100 BCE depicts a group of warriors.

This ancient Greek sculpture depicts a man carrying a calf. Much of Bronze Age Greek life revolved around farming.

tombs, and because the form was usually female, it is thought they may represent goddesses who would protect the dead. They could also have been votive figures (objects of prayer).

The first modern discoveries of Cycladic figurines were made in the 1880s CE. In the early 20th century CE, the statuettes became fashionable with art collectors who admired them for their purity and simplicity of form.

Cultural developments

This Early Cycladic era is divided into two separate periods: Early Cycladic I (c. 3200–2700 BCE) and Early Cycladic II (c. 2700–2400 BCE), based on significant burial-site finds at Grotta-Pelos and Keros-Syros, respectively. Besides the female figurines, other artifacts found in tombs of this Early Cycladic period include a seated male marble figure, depicted playing a musical instrument, plus items such as bowls, bottles, and vases. Because the quality and quantity of goods vary from grave to grave, archaeologists believe that different levels of society were beginning to be seen on the Cyclades at this time.

As well as the beautiful white marble of the Cyclades, another substance of benefit to the whole region was obsidian. This black, glassy volcanic rock was found on Milos and was prized for making knives or scraping tools. The islanders were able to profit by trading in obsidian.

Moving inland

A significant shift in the population of the Cyclades took place around 2500 BCE. The communities that had been living in simple villages close to the coasts to facilitate their fishing activities started to move into the central parts of the islands and to build citadels, making the people less vulnerable to attack. One particular citadel, found at Kastri on Syros, was encircled by a wall with six towers.

From around 2000 BCE, the grave goods become more sophisticated, and it is thought that the Cycladic islanders may have had contact with, and been influenced by, the Minoan civilization that was developing on the nearby island of Crete. In more than 500 tombs excavated near Kastri, terra-cotta, marble, and gold vessels have been found, along with pins made of bronze and silver that were probably used to fasten garments. The fact that these pins are engraved with designs also found in Egypt and mainland Greece suggests that the Cycladic islanders were regularly trading with those countries.

Volcanic eruption

Some time around 1500 BCE (or possibly earlier; see box, page 168), a volcano on the southerly island of Thera (present-day Santorini) erupted with cataclysmic

DELOS

The island of Delos figures in many Greek legends. The very creation of the island was the subject of a myth. Poseidon, the god of the sea, together with Zeus, king of the gods, was supposed to have used columns made of diamonds to secure an enormous rock to the sea bed; this rock became Delos. Delos was destined to be the birthplace of the moon goddess Artemis and her twin brother, the sun god Apollo, who was also the god of poetry and music and is often depicted holding a lyre (a form of small harp).

When the Ionians occupied the Cyclades, they designated the island of Delos as their religious capital, because they believed themselves to be descended from Apollo. By the eighth century BCE, a large religious festival dedicated to Apollo was being held annually on Delos.

results. Ash and volcanic debris rained down on Thera and the surrounding islands. The explosion was so violent that it actually split Thera into several pieces, resulting in one large island and several smaller ones; much of the original island disappeared into the sea. Volcanic debris was lifted high into the atmosphere and deposited thousand of miles away.

One town that was devastated by the eruption was Akrotiri. As the volcano exploded, enormous boulders

Cycladic art is highly distinctive. This statuette from around 2600 BCE depicts a woman standing with her arms folded.

THE EXPLOSION AT THERA

The volcanic eruption on the island of Thera was one of the major events to occur in the Mediterranean region in the second millennium BCE. Ash from the explosion was thrown so far into the sky that some of it has been found in Greenland and North America. The eruption would have caused huge tidal waves to crash into other Aegean islands, including Crete, which is why the aftereffects of the explosion have sometimes been blamed for the downfall of the Minoan civilization.

Traditionally, the date of the Thera eruption has been placed at around 1500 BCE. That date was originally put forward in 1939 because pottery found buried by the eruption on Thera closely resembled Egyptian pottery from 1500 BCE. For several decades, this theory was acknowledged to be true. However, from the 1970s onward, archaeologists increasingly began to dispute the date, as radiocarbon evidence began to suggest that the disaster may have occurred much earlier, around 1625 BCE.

In 2006, a new theory was proposed in an article published in the magazine *Science*. Research by Danish geologist Walter Friedrich suggested that the eruption occurred between 1627 and 1600 BCE. Friedrich's conclusion was based on radiocarbon dating of an olive branch that was buried in the lava. Friedrich's theory did not settle the argument, however. While many geologists and archaeologists have supported his claims, others have questioned his findings.

The island of Santorini, called Thera in ancient times, is now a popular tourist destination.

came crashing down on the town and the sky darkened with ash. Next, tons of molten lava engulfed the hapless town, which was buried under 16 feet (5 m) of debris and so preserved almost intact, rather like the later Roman town of Pompeii.

Cycladic life

When Thera was eventually excavated, it gave a very clear picture of what life was like in the Cyclades before around 1500 BCE. The people lived in houses consisting of several rooms, arranged on either two or three stories. The narrow streets of the town were equipped with a simple drainage system for removing sewage. The houses contained wooden furniture and pottery and, on the ground floor, large earthenware jars for storing foodstuffs such as grain, vegetables, dried fish, wine, and oil.

One room in each house was arranged as a shrine and decorated with wall paintings (frescoes) showing landscapes with animals, birds, and flowers such as lilies and crocuses. In other houses excavated at Phylakope on Milos, frescoes have been found depicting battles, festivals, and, in one famous painting, a school of flying fish.

Because no human remains have been found at Thera, it is thought that the inhabitants may have had time to escape, but where they went is a mystery. Another mystery linked to Thera is that of the lost world of Atlantis, which was the subject of later Greek legends. It has been thought that these legends may refer to Thera.

End of Cycladic culture

From around 1500 BCE, the Cyclades came increasingly under the influence of the Mycenaeans on mainland Greece, and Cycladic culture was gradually absorbed into that of the Mycenaeans. The Cyclades were also in contact with the Phoenicians,

who visited the islands to trade for precious metals. By around 1000 BCE, the Cycladic culture had completely disappeared. Most of the islands had been settled by Ionians from Anatolia, while Dorians from northwestern Greece had occupied Milos and Thera.

See also:

The Bronze Age (volume 1, page 32) • The Minoans (volume 2, page 170) • Mycenae and Troy (volume 2, page 182) • The Phoenicians (volume 2, page 196)

Two young boys box in this fresco found in the town of Akrotiri.

THE MINOANS

TIME LINE

c. 3000 BCE

People living in Aegean begin to make bronze by mixing copper and tin; dawn of Minoan culture on Crete.

c. 2000 BCE

First large palace complexes built at Knossos and Phaistos.

c. 1700 BCE

Early palaces destroyed, either by invaders or by an earthquake; later rebuilt.

c. 1525 BCE

Kings based at Knossos reach height of power.

c. 1500 BCE

Volcanic eruption on nearby island of Thera results in vast quantities of ash showered over Crete.

c. 1450 BCE

Minoan civilization comes to end. Palaces burned down, possibly by Mycenaean invaders.

The Minoan culture, which flourished on Crete between around 2500 and 1450 BCE, was one of the first major cultures to emerge in Europe. Much of what is known about the Minoans has been gained through excavations at Knossos.

In the spring of 1900 CE, there was great excitement on the island of Crete in the Mediterranean Sea. British archaeologist Arthur Evans and his team had just unearthed the first signs of a sophisticated Bronze Age civilization on the island. The excavations were centered on a large mound, called Kephala (or Knossos), in the north of the island. Local legend had it that this was the site of a great palace belonging to the mythical King Minos. According to the legend, Minos's palace was home to a monster known as the Minotaur, which lived in a labyrinth and devoured young men and women as sacrificial victims (see box, page 176).

The first finds were fragments of pottery decorated with images of sea creatures such as starfish, dolphins, sea urchins, and octopuses. The subject matter of the designs suggested that the pottery was produced by a seagoing people. Even more exciting were the fragments of a wall painting that showed a man in a loincloth carrying a vase. Similarly clothed figures had been painted on the walls of ancient Egyptian tombs, where they were identified as the Keftiu (island people) paying tribute to the pharaoh. It seemed that the Cretans and the Keftiu could have been one and the same.

Very soon, evidence of walls, floors, and columns came to light, indicating the presence of an enormous palace extending over 6 acres (2.4 ha). Evans named it the Palace of Minos (see box, page 174). The 1,400 rooms, which included ceremonial chambers, were connected by corridors and staircases, and many of the walls were decorated with elaborate paintings showing young men and women and more sea creatures. There were also paintings of bulls, suggesting that the palace was indeed the source of the Minotaur legend.

The site that Evans had discovered was the center of a Bronze Age culture that flourished on Crete from around 2500 to 1450 BCE. It was the first sophisticated civilization to develop in Europe; it was a civilization centered on trade and an efficient bureaucracy, and unlike most other early civilizations, it seemed entirely unwarlike. Prior to the Minoans (as Evans called these people), life on Crete had been primitive.

The Neolithic period

Before around 6000 BCE, Crete may have been uninhabited, but in the sixth millennium BCE, groups of people from Anatolia settled in mainland Greece and on Crete, bringing with them a knowledge of farming. These early

This mosaic depicts the Greek hero Theseus killing the Minotaur. According to legend, the Minotaur lived in a maze on Crete.

Cretan settlers found a large island (the fifth largest in the Mediterranean) with mountains covered in trees and a large fertile plain in the center. The warm climate made it a favorable area for growing crops. The farmers grew barley, oats, and wheat, as well as pulses and peas. They kept goats, sheep, cattle, and pigs and supplemented their diet by hunting and fishing. They fashioned pots out of clay by hand and made axes and chisels from stones that they ground to a sharp edge.

The Bronze Age

Around 3000 BCE, people living in the region of the Aegean discovered how to make bronze by mixing copper with tin, so beginning the period known as the Bronze Age. The people living on Crete in the early Bronze Age built houses of mud bricks. The houses had separate living rooms, kitchens, and workrooms. The Cretans became skilled metalworkers, producing beautiful jewelry in gold and silver.

At the same time that the Minoan civilization was developing on Crete, other cultures were developing in different parts of the Mediterranean region. One culture arose on a group of islands in the Aegean called the Cyclades. The early inhabitants of the Cyclades are most famous for the finely wrought figurines that they carved out of stone. The Greek mainland saw the rise of another culture, the Helladic, which in its later stages was known as the Mycenaean civilization.

When Arthur Evans was excavating the palace at Knossos, he divided Minoan history up into three main periods:

This ivory figurine was found in the palace at Knossos. It dates to around the 17th century BCE.

Early Minoan (3000–2000 BCE), Middle Minoan (2000–1600 BCE), and Late Minoan (1600–1050 BCE). However, other historians have chosen to divide Minoan history into three alternate periods spanning a shorter time: First Palace (1900–1700 BCE), Second Palace (1650–1540 BCE), and Third Palace (1450–1200 BCE).

During the Early Minoan period, the Minoans started to use bronze to make metal tools such as daggers, adzes, and double-headed axes. They grew olives and grape vines and traded the resulting olive oil and wine with neighboring peoples in the Aegean, taking to the sea in ships propelled by a combination of oars and square sails attached to masts. The Minoans used seals to stamp impressions on wet clay, possibly to seal storage jars to guard against theft. They also began building extensive settlements, although few traces of them now remain.

The age of the palaces

It was in the Middle Minoan period that the Minoans started to build great palaces at sites such as Knossos, Phaistos, Mallia, and Zakro. These palaces consisted of a complex of buildings surrounding a large open court and the main royal residence. The buildings, which served as the island's administrative center, included workshops for craftsmen and artisans, plus special storage rooms for oil, wine, grain, and other farming produce.

The first palaces have disappeared almost completely, but there have been numerous smaller finds from this period.

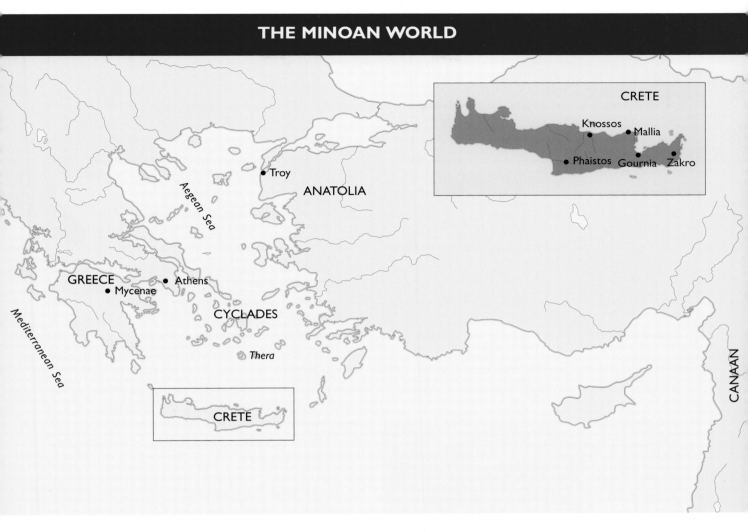

THE MINOAN WORLD

One of the most striking of these finds is a type of thin-walled pottery called Kamares ware, which was produced on a potter's wheel and decorated with spirals and plant motifs in red, orange, yellow, and white on a blue-black background. This refined pottery was crafted by specialized potters both for the domestic market and for export.

A collection of small plaques found in the palace at Knossos gives a good idea of the architecture of this period. The plaques are made of faience (a fine grade of pottery covered with a glaze) and depict city houses built of stone, bound together with large wooden beams. All the houses have a least two floors and a flat roof, and many appear to have a small central court that possibly served as an air and light shaft. Some of the houses are shown with window openings painted bright red, which might indicate that the early inhabitants of Crete used oiled parchment as an early type of windowpane.

The palace at Knossos

Around 1700 BCE, all the Minoan palaces were destroyed, either by earthquakes or invaders. They were all soon rebuilt, however. The new palace at Knossos became even more elaborate than its predecessor, with at least three stories and many rooms, including a magnificent throne room. The kings of Knossos reached the peak of their power

THE PALACE OF MINOS

The Palace of Minos excavated by Arthur Evans at Knossos is one of the most fascinating archaeological sites of the ancient world. The site covers a vast area around 3 miles (5 km) from the north coast of Crete, and it is thought that as many as 30,000 people lived and worked there in its heyday.

Digging down, Evans discovered a palace five stories high in places, with the floors connected by a grand staircase. The whole palace was skillfully designed to let light in and allow air to circulate—and to protect the occupants from the fierce summer heat. In winter, the doors would be closed so that fireplaces could provide warmth.

One very grand room was the throne room, which opened off the central courtyard. Inside

was a stately throne carved out of gypsum and backed by a colorful mural depicting griffins (a kind of mythical animal). Evans thought that this room might have been used by the king to receive visitors, although others have suggested it might have been used for religious ceremonies.

The eastern side of the palace contained the royal apartments. The king's room was a large double room with a light well at one end and a veranda facing east. Motifs of double axes were carved on stone blocks found in the room, and for this reason it was named the Hall of the Double Axes. The queen's hall was decorated with paintings of dolphins and a dancing girl. It contained a bathroom in one corner, with an earthenware bathtub that was probably filled by servants. A hole in the floor leading to the drains made emptying it simple. In an adjoining room, there was a toilet. This was simply a hole in a stone slab with a drain beneath that carried the waste away to a stream.

As well as these grand rooms, there was a multitude of smaller rooms, all connected by corridors and staircases, together with vast numbers of underground storage rooms for the goods brought in from the surrounding countryside. The palace was a hive of activity. In addition to the king, queen, and nobles, there were priests, storekeepers, accountants and scribes, plus many servants and slaves. In the workshops around the palace, there were craftspeople such as jewelers, painters, potters, and carpenters busily plying their trade to produce the wonderful artifacts of the Minoan culture.

A pithos, or storage jar, stands amid the excavated ruins of the palace at Knossos. The palace complex at Knossos contained many storage rooms that would have contained pithoi such as this. Pithoi were usually used as containers for wine and olive oil.

between around 1550 and 1500 BCE, dominating the Aegean region and trading extensively with the Greek mainland, the Aegean islands, Anatolia (present-day Turkey), Egypt, and the Canaanite Syrian coast.

The basic plan at Knossos—which was echoed in the other palaces—was that of a large central courtyard surrounded by reception halls, living quarters, workshops, and storerooms. The palace was not protected by fortifications, and its western side looked out over wide agoras (public courtyards used for ceremonies and gatherings). The whole palace was supplied with water through an elaborate system of pipes, while drains and conduits removed waste water and sewage from the site. The storerooms at Knossos are particularly striking. They were long, narrow basement rooms containing rows of enormous storage jars called *pithoi* in which grain, oil, and wine were kept.

Social structure

Minoan society was divided into several regions and groups. Presiding over the country as a whole was the king. Below the king were the nobles, who were provincial rulers living in country mansions. A group of officials controlled the operations of the merchants, who contributed to the region's wealth through trade. In particular, merchants supplied imported materials such as ivory to the craftsmen who lived and worked in the palace. Below these classes came the farmers, who produced the agricultural goods that were so important for the

This artist's illustration depicts how the palace at Knossos may have looked. The palace was spread over a large area and contained several floors.

THE LEGEND OF THE MINOTAUR

According to Greek mythology, the god Poseidon sent a snow-white bull to King Minos of Crete, intending that the king should sacrifice the bull to Poseidon. When Minos refused to do this, Poseidon, in revenge, made Pasiphaë, the wife of Minos and queen of Crete, fall in love with the bull. As a result of this affair, she bore a child—a monster with a human body and a bull's head—that was called the Minotaur.

To keep the Minotaur safe, Minos commissioned the architect Daedalus to build a labyrinth so complex that nobody could find the way through it. When the maze was completed, the Minotaur was locked inside.

When the son of Minos was murdered by the king of Athens, Minos demanded that every nine years Athens should send seven young men and seven young women to Minos in compensation. These young people were fed to the Minotaur. Finally, the Athenian hero Theseus decided to put an end to this practice. He offered himself as one of the victims and sailed with the others to Crete. Ariadne, the daughter of Minos, fell in love with Theseus and offered to help him escape his fate. She gave him a ball of thread, which he tied to the entrance to the maze and unwound as he went. At the center of the maze, he found the Minotaur asleep and killed him. Then, with the help of the thread, Theseus made his escape, together with the intended victims he had rescued.

This drinking vessel made in the shape of a bull's head was found at Knossos. It was made between around 1900 and 1400 BCE.

Minoans' wealth. There was also a class of scribes, who were kept busy recording stocks of produce on clay tablets.

The Minoans had a highly developed religious life, and many priests and priestesses lived in the palaces. Rather than building temples to their gods, the Minoans held religious ceremonies in their houses, at hilltop shrines, or in special rooms in the palaces. Many gods and goddesses were worshipped, but it seems that one goddess, the mother (or earth) goddess, was supreme. She watched over animals and plants and symbolized fertility. Every year, she married a young god who died when winter came around but who came back to life in the spring. Another important goddess was the snake goddess. Usually portrayed holding a snake in each hand, she was seen as the guardian of the house.

Many replicas of bull's horns carved in stone have been found in Crete, suggesting that the bull played an important part in some religious cult. There are also several wall paintings that show young men and women somersaulting over a charging bull. This sport possibly took place in the palace courtyard and may have been part of a religious ritual.

Minoan towns and villas

Minoan palaces were encircled by large cities, which were connected to each other and to other Cretan towns by paved roads. One famous Minoan town is Gournia, which stands on a ridge overlooking the sea around 38 miles (60 km) east of Knossos. This town, excavated at around the same time as Knossos, consisted of a maze of winding streets connecting small square houses and courtyards. The houses were up to three stories and had flat roofs. The first floor usually contained workshops or storerooms, while the living quarters were on the second floor, which was reached by an outside staircase. From the tools found in the workshops, it is clear that the town's inhabitants included potters, weavers, metalsmiths, and carpenters, as well as fishermen and farmers.

A number of villas have also been excavated on Crete, and they were all built to the same plan as the palaces,

Athletes are shown vaulting over a charging bull in this fresco from the east wing of the palace at Knossos. Experts are divided over whether bull leaping was a religious ritual or just a dangerous sport.

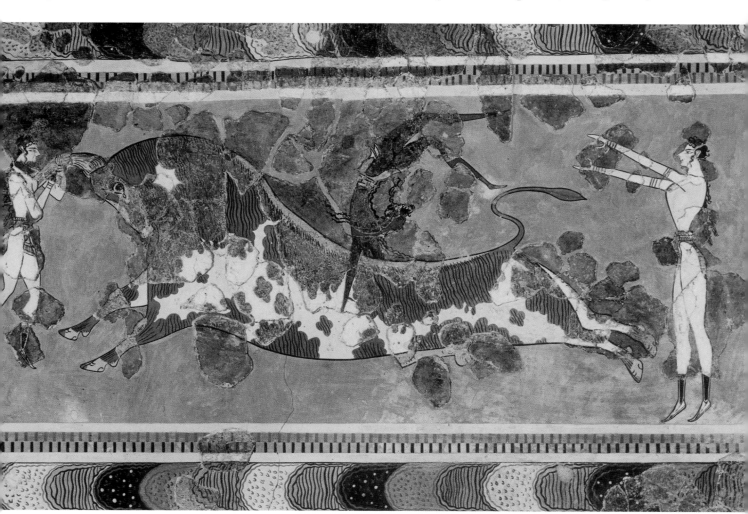

The remains of the Minoan town of Gournia are extremely well preserved. Like a number of other Minoan towns, Gournia was the site of a large palace.

THE PALACES AT PHAISTOS

Knossos was just one of the many locations where Minoan palaces were built. Another location was Phaistos, in the south of the island. The site was occupied by around 4000 BCE, but the first palace at Phaistos was not built until around 2000 BCE, roughly the same time as the palace at Knossos. What is now known as the "old palace" at Phaistos was destroyed by fire around 1700 BCE. Another palace was built in its place.

Like the palace at Knossos, the "new palace" at Phaistos was built around a magnificent central courtyard, lined with pillars. The royal quarters stood to the north. Workshops were found to the east, while storerooms were located to the west. The west wing also contained rooms that were used for religious purposes; religious figurines were found there and pictures of double axheads (a religious motif) were carved into the walls. Like the other great palaces, the palace at Phaistos was destroyed around 1450 BCE when the Minoan civilization came to an end.

albeit on a smaller scale. Some historians believe that these villas, which are all located within 7 to 10 miles (11 to 16 km) of each other, were the regional offices of a central power.

Minoan art

The interiors of the palaces were decorated with colorful murals, some made up of abstract patterns, others depicting plants, animals, and people. These paintings are often called frescoes, but true frescoes are painted on wet plaster, whereas the Minoan murals were painted on dry plaster walls. The so-called House of the Frescoes at Knossos is famous for its murals showing a park where various flowering plants are complemented by high-spouting fountains and a blue bird. Murals showing dolphins and flying fish have been found in several other places.

The paintings of men and women provide a clear idea of how the Minoans looked and dressed. When taking part in rituals, men often covered their bodies with a type of red powder for ceremonial purposes, so the men are often shown painted red. Men usually wore their hair long, but were clean shaven. In some paintings, men are shown wearing just a leather belt and a loincloth, while in others they wear a kilt. Women wore dresses with a long flounced skirt and an open bodice that left their breasts and arms bare, their jewelry consisted of rings, bracelets, necklaces, and earrings, and they had elaborate hair-styles with strings of beads braided into their long hair.

Women often occupy a prominent position in these paintings. They are shown dominating ceremonies from a place of honor and performing dances in beautiful costumes. In the famous bull-leaping fresco at Knossos, two young women are shown taking equal part with a young man in the ceremony.

This fresco probably shows a Minoan priestess. The woman depicted is sometimes known as La Parisienne because she resembles the subjects of paintings by French artist Henri Toulouse-Lautrec.

MINOAN WRITING

The Minoans were one of the earliest peoples to develop writing. From around 2000 BCE onward, they began using a system of hieroglyphic or pictographic writing, with signs in the shape of animals or objects. This form of picture writing may have originated through contact with the Egyptians, who were also writing in hieroglyphics at this time. Nevertheless, very few of the Minoan signs resemble those of the Egyptians.

Around 300 years later, the Minoans started writing in a simplified linear script, which used signs to represent the different syllables in a word. This script was usually scratched on clay tablets, although there is evidence that some kind of paper (perhaps similar to the papyrus of the Egyptians) was also used, together with a form of ink. Tablets in this script found at Knossos bear stockkeeping records of textiles, grain, animals, oils, and spices. Arthur Evans named this script Linear A.

No large statues from the Minoan civilization have survived, but the pedestals of what were presumably wooden statues have been preserved. A number of small statues have been found. These are made of ivory (sometimes inlaid with gold), bronze, or faience, and they depict goddesses or priestesses, praying figures, acrobats, animals, and a few tableaus, such as a stable with cattle or a group of dancers. Occasionally, children are portrayed.

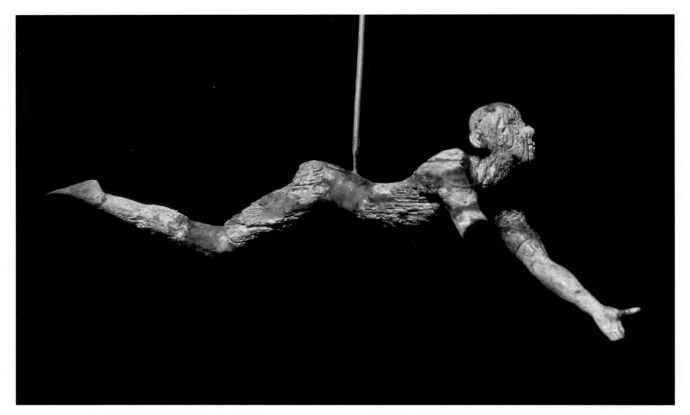

This ivory figurine depicts a Minoan acrobat taking part in a bull-leaping ritual. The figurine was found in the palace at Knossos and was made around 1550 BCE.

HUMAN SACRIFICE

It seems clear that some religious rituals practiced by the Minoans involved the slaughter of animals as a sacrifice to the gods. However, there may have been an even more dramatic and sinister practice. In 1979, a major sanctuary was excavated in the mountains around 4.5 miles (7.2 km) south of Knossos. Among the items found were a cult statue and a number of votive offerings. What caused the greatest excitement was evidence that when the sanctuary was destroyed by an earthquake, a human sacrifice had been in progress. The body of a young man found tied to a low altar had died as a result of having his throat cut. Other finds in Knossos have included children's bones that show knife marks, suggesting that child sacrifice took place—or even cannibalism. There have been further archaeological indications to support the idea that these were not isolated instances.

The pots and ceramic ware from this period show that there was a great technical and artistic tradition. Motifs from the plant kingdom, inherited from the earlier Kamares ware, were mingled with images of marine creatures. These decorations were painted in dark colors on a light background.

It is obvious from a number of other found items that sections of Minoan society were very affluent. Beautiful jewelry was wrought in gold, while elegant stone vases were made of rock crystal, obsidian (a kind of volcanic glass), alabaster, or marble. Gold signet rings engraved with scenes of rituals have also been found.

Other important sources of information on Minoan life are the numerous seals that have been found. They were engraved with many designs, including geometric patterns and representations of human beings and animals. After 2000 BCE, the seals bear a type of writing that Arthur Evans termed hieroglyphic. Three

centuries later, this writing was replaced by a simplified script called Linear A (see box, page 179). Seals were used for placing a personal or official stamp on objects as a signature. They were also used as ornaments and charms.

The Third Palace period

Around the 15th century BCE, the Minoan people suffered a series of disasters. At the beginning of the century, the volcano on the island of Thera in the Cyclades erupted violently, causing catastrophic destruction over a wide area. Around 50 years later, many Minoan centers were destroyed by fire, and the palaces and other settlements may have been ransacked before being put to the

torch. Whatever the reason, the existing social order was overthrown.

Invaders, probably Greek-speaking Mycenaeans from the mainland, came to dominate Crete. They made Knossos, which had suffered relatively little damage, their administrative center, but by 1300 BCE, the town appears to have been destroyed by unknown attackers. Occupied by the Mycenaeans, Crete became a Greek city-state, and the Minoan civilization that had flourished for more than 1,000 years was at an end.

See also:

Bronze Age Greece (volume 2, page 162) • Mycenae and Troy (volume 2, page 182)

This fresco depicts a Minoan ship entering a port. The Minoans were highly successful traders.

MYCENAE AND TROY

TIME LINE

c. 3000 BCE

First settlement appears at Troy.

c. 1600 BCE

Mycenae becomes major power on Greek mainland.

c. 1450 BCE

Mycenaeans invade Crete, making Knossos administrative center; fortress at Tiryns built around this time.

c. 1275 BCE

Tomb known as Treasury of Atreus built at Mycenae.

c. 1250 BCE

Mycenaean era comes to end, possibly as result of invasion from the north. Troy VIIa, the Troy of Homer, destroyed.

c. 1050 BCE

Troy VIIb destroyed; city abandoned for several centuries.

The Mycenaean civilization was the first major culture to develop on the Greek mainland. It flourished from around 1600 BCE until around 1250 BCE. According to legend, a major rival of the Mycenaean kingdoms was the Anatolian city of Troy.

Around the same time that the Minoan civilization was flourishing on Crete, another culture was developing on the Greek mainland. This new culture was the Mycenaean culture, which was named after the ancient city of Mycenae, one of the culture's centers. The Mycenaean civilization was not a single kingdom; it consisted of a group of city-states united by a common language and way of life. Other great centers of Mycenaean society were the cities of Athens, Thebes, Pylos, Tiryns, and Gla.

Unlike the Minoans, the Mycenaeans were a warlike people. However, they were also successful traders and skillful craftsmen. Their origins are still a mystery. Some historians believe they were a Greek-speaking people from the northeast who migrated to mainland Greece around 2000 BCE. Other experts, while accepting that such people did arrive in Greece, remain unconvinced that they were the Mycenaeans. Wherever they came from, the Mycenaeans had become a major power in the Aegean region by 1600 BCE. They were to dominate the region for the next 400 years. Around 1450 BCE, they invaded Crete, where they made the city of Knossos their administrative center. They also occupied many other Aegean islands and their commercial empire extended throughout the Mediterranean region.

Most of the knowledge about the Mycenaeans is of fairly recent origin. The obsession of a German archaeologist, Heinrich Schliemann (1822–1890), with the story of Troy led to the city of Mycenae being discovered in the 19th century CE. That Mycenaeans spoke Greek was only established in 1952, when a cryptographer succeeded in deciphering the script on clay tablets that had been found at Pylos and Mycenae (see box, page 186).

Schliemann and Homer

The epic poems the *Iliad* and the *Odyssey*, attributed to the Greek poet Homer, describe a Greek world in which Agamemnon ruled Mycenae, the paramount Greek city, while his brother Menelaus was king of Sparta and Pylos and Ithaca were ruled by Nestor and Odysseus respectively. Both of these epics were once regarded as complete fiction, but historians now accept that they give some very valuable glimpses into the Mycenaean civilization of the 12th century BCE.

In the late 19th century CE, nothing was known about Greek history prior to 800 BCE, but Heinrich Schliemann became convinced that the world described by Homer was based on fact and that Troy and Mycenae had really existed. In 1876, Schliemann set out to

prove that Mycenae was the city of Agamemnon. While excavating a burial ground close to the ruins of Mycenae, Schliemann came across a tomb containing many exquisite gold objects, including a gold death mask—a replica of a dead person's facial features. Schliemann was convinced he had found the tomb of the Mycenaean king. "I have looked upon the face of Agamemnon," he declared triumphantly in a telegram written to the king of Greece. Schliemann was mistaken, however. It

Dating from the 16th century BCE, this gold death mask was discovered in a shaft burial at Mycenae. At the time, it was mistakenly believed to have belonged to the legendary king Agamemnon.

has since been established that the mask dates from the 1550s BCE, around 300 years before the time of the Trojan War.

The city of Mycenae

Like many other cities in the ancient world, Mycenae had been built on a hill to make it easy to defend if attacked. At the top of the hill was the upper city, or citadel, which contained the royal palace. During the Late Mycenaean period (c. 1550–1100 BCE), the citadel was surrounded by a defensive wall almost half a mile (805 m) long, 30 feet (9.1 m) high, and at least 20 feet (6.1 m) thick. The wall was constructed of massive limestone blocks so heavy that later generations believed the wall must have been built by the Cyclopes, a mythical race of one-eyed giants. As a consequence, this type of masonry is called Cyclopean.

On the west side of the fortress, the Lion Gate, the main gateway into the city, was an impressive structure, crowned by two stone lions standing on their hind legs on either side of a column. The lions are thought to have been a symbol of kingship. The gate was closed by a set of double doors, and the spindle holes for these doors can still be seen in the threshold and the massive lintel. The doors were hung on the spindle ends that protruded from the holes. A feature of the gate that seems to bring the ancient city to life is the fact that the threshold still shows traces of wear from the constant passage of chariots and carts.

HEINRICH SCHLIEMANN

Heinrich Schliemann, born in January 1822, in Germany, was the son of an impoverished pastor. Schliemann left school at 14 and, after a succession of odd jobs, sailed for California, where he made a fortune during the Gold Rush. Schliemann next established himself in Russia, where he became a successful businessman and eventually grew rich enough to retire in his late thirties, devoting himself to archaeology.

Schliemann had been obsessed with the stories of the Trojan War since childhood, and he used the fortune that he had amassed to pursue his dream. He not only excavated the cities of Troy and Mycenae, but also the city of Tiryns. Schliemann publicized his discoveries through books and letters to British newspapers.

Schliemann died in Naples on December 26, 1890, as the result of an ear infection.

At the center of the citadel lies the palace, which covers an area of 200 by 180 feet (61 by 55 m). Built on uneven terrain, the palace probably gave the impression of being a stepped or terraced structure. The entrance to the palace was approached by a grand staircase, some of which still survives.

A royal residence

The palace was an enormously important building. Besides housing the royal family, it acted as a regional center and a military headquarters. In addition to a throne room, the palace contained halls, storerooms, and workshops. The core room was the megaron—a large rectangular room where the king presided over state business. This audience chamber had a large central hearth where a fire was kept burning, and the walls were painted with colorful scenes of daily life.

The citadel, which contained several houses as well as the palace, had many underground vaults and a system of underground drains. A reliable water supply was crucial to the city, particularly in time of siege, and Mycenae had a secret underground reservoir outside the wall of the citadel. Historians believe that the water was brought into the citadel by an underground channel.

In addition to the king and his relatives, the citadel housed a number of other noble families, probably in separate houses. Most of the houses were spacious and had two stories. In the late 1960s, a sanctuary containing the remains of terra-cotta figures 2 feet (0.6 m) high was found within the walls. These figures were possibly cult statues.

From the remains of a number of dwellings found on the hillside outside the citadel, it has been assumed that a substantial town extended from the foot of the city walls. In times of war, the population of the town would have taken refuge within the citadel.

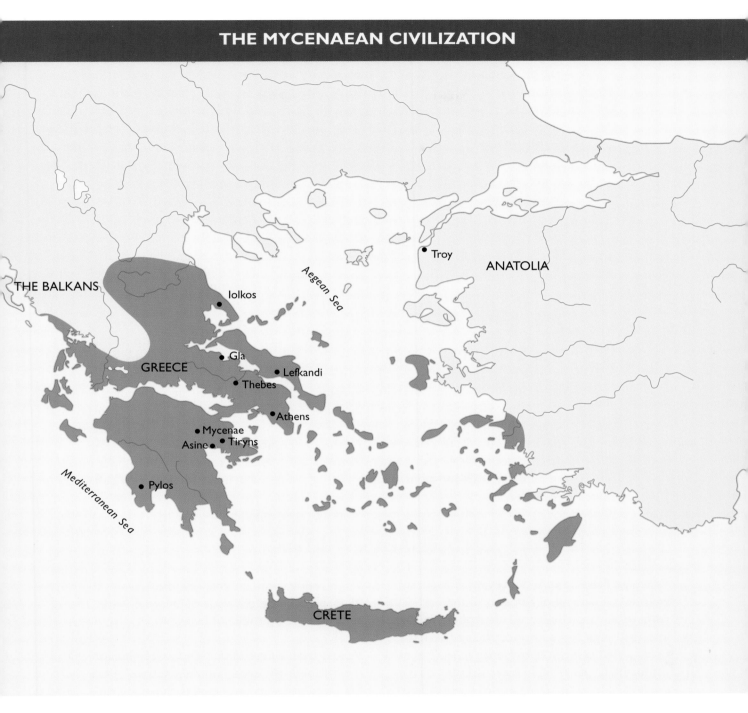

THE MYCENAEAN CIVILIZATION

THE BALKANS

GREECE

Aegean Sea

Mediterranean Sea

ANATOLIA

- Troy
- Iolkos
- Gla
- Lefkandi
- Thebes
- Athens
- Mycenae
- Asine
- Tiryns
- Pylos

CRETE

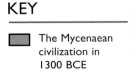

KEY

The Mycenaean civilization in 1300 BCE

Tombs

Two styles of Mycenaean tombs have been discovered. When Schliemann was excavating Mycenae, he found an extensive burial site in the northwest corner of the citadel. Archaeologists call this location Grave Circle A. The site contains a number of royal tombs dating from around 1600 BCE. These tombs were composed of simple shafts, which were dug deep into the ground. Each tomb contained the bodies of several generations of royalty, together with their possessions. When a tomb was full, it would be covered with stones and the shaft filled with earth. Later, a second circle of shaft tombs, called Grave Circle B, was discovered outside the citadel walls.

The treasures that were buried with the deceased in these shaft tombs are a testimony to the power and wealth of Mycenae in those days. As well as gold death masks, the graves yielded many richly decorated weapons, including a number of daggers inlaid with gold or silver. Some of the daggers featured entire scenes, including hunts and battles, depicted in inlay work. The hilts of the daggers were often made of wood or bone to which reliefs of hammered gold were applied.

The deceased were not only provided with weapons, however. A number of other splendid objects have also been found in the burial shafts. These objects include vases, dishes, golden *rhytons* (an ornate type of drinking vessel), beautifully crafted diadems, earrings, hairpins, necklaces, and bracelets, as well as hundreds of tiny gold disks, which were probably used to decorate clothes. Archaeologists have also found a number of cylinder seals and signet rings.

Another type of Mycenaean tomb was the *tholos* tomb, which was used from around 1500 BCE. These more elaborate tombs were built by master craftsmen. Schliemann excavated many of these tombs, which appear to have been reserved for the elite. The *tholos* tomb had a dome-shaped roof, and because of the domed appearance, the tombs are also known as beehive tombs.

In a *tholos* tomb, the burial space consisted of a round hole in the ground covered by a dome of stone blocks. The blocks were laid in such a way that each layer protruded inward over the layer below, leaving only a small opening at the top. The opening was then closed with an apex stone. The stone blocks were covered with soil and pebbles, and the mound thus created was given an identifying mark or gravestone. Inside the tomb, the protruding portions of the stone blocks were removed, and the surface was smoothed, creating a conical dome.

A *tholos* tomb was often built into the side of a hill and was approached by a

MYCENAEAN WRITING

When archaeologist Arthur Evans was excavating the Minoan city of Knossos in the early 20th century, he unearthed a number of clay tablets inscribed with three distinct types of script. Evans called these scripts hieroglyphic (the earliest form), Linear A, and Linear B. Evans never succeeded in deciphering any of these scripts.

In 1939, excavations at the Mycenaean palace at Pylos turned up many more Linear B tablets, and thousands more were subsequently found at Mycenae, Tiryns, and Thebes. Using the tablets from Pylos and Knossos, a cryptographer, Michael Ventris, set about deciphering Linear B in the 1950s. Most people believed that the script represented an unknown language of the Minoans, because the signs of Linear B were clearly based on those of Linear A.

Ventris tried to establish a phonetic value for the syllable signs, based on assumptions about the place names on the tablets. Starting from such names as Konoso and Aminiso (Knossos and Amnissos), Ventris was able to uncover an archaic form of Greek. In 1953, together with John Chadwick, a specialist in Greek historical linguistics, Ventris published his findings. The initial article was controversial, but the decipherment is now generally accepted—the language of the Mycenaeans was Greek.

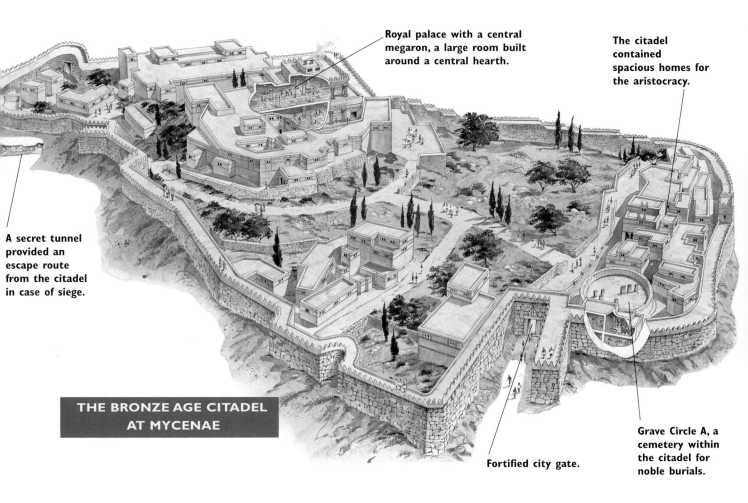

Royal palace with a central megaron, a large room built around a central hearth.

The citadel contained spacious homes for the aristocracy.

A secret tunnel provided an escape route from the citadel in case of siege.

THE BRONZE AGE CITADEL AT MYCENAE

Fortified city gate.

Grave Circle A, a cemetery within the citadel for noble burials.

long open corridor called a *dromos*. One particularly splendid *tholos* tomb discovered in the citadel of Mycenae was named the Treasury of Atreus (see box, page 188).

Other Mycenaean centers

Although Mycenae was the mightiest center of the Mycenaean world, other royal fortresses and palaces of similar or even greater size were built at Tiryns, Asine, Pylos, Athens, Thebes, and Iolkos.

At Tiryns, a fortress was built in three stages some time after 1450 BCE. This fortress has mighty walls that surpass those of Mycenae both in height and in the size of their stone blocks. Several palace buildings, including a megaron,

have been found in Tiryns. Probably the most striking features of these buildings are the covered corridors and casements enclosing impressive galleries.

The floorplan of one building, Nestor's Palace at Pylos, has been particularly well preserved. Named after one of the city's semimythical kings, Nestor's Palace comprised several buildings, which were not protected by massive surrounding walls but were probably guarded by fortresses along the coast. At the gateway to the citadel, there was a guardroom, as well as another room where records were kept of the daily business of the palace, produce received in taxes, and work to be carried out by officials. At the center of the citadel was

This artist's illustration depicts how the citadel of Mycenae may have appeared.

THE TREASURY OF ATREUS

The so-called Treasury of Atreus was a huge, handsome domed grave at Mycenae that dates from the early 13th century BCE. Atreus was a mythical king of Mycenae who was involved in a bitter and tragic battle with his brother Thyestes for the city's throne. The identity of the real-life king who was buried in the tomb remains a mystery, however.

One of the most spectacular features of the dome is its impressive *dromos* (entrance passage), which measures 120 feet (36.6 m) long and 20 feet (6.1 m) wide. This *dromos* leads up to a majestic doorway that is 30 feet (9.1 m) tall and would have been elaborately decorated. A gigantic stone block weighing 120 tons (5,443 kg) closes off the top of the entrance. Inside the tomb, the vast dome has a diameter and height of approximately 45 feet (13.7 m) each and consists of 33 layers of stone blocks fitted snugly together. Remnants of bronze nails suggest that the inside of the dome may well have been decorated with bronze rosettes and friezes.

Using evidence from this and other tombs, archaeologists have tried to imagine what a royal funeral would have been like. It probably started with the funeral procession—consisting of the body of the king drawn on a chariot, followed by priests and mourners—moving slowly along the *dromos* toward the entrance to the tomb, where great doors of bronze would open to admit the procession. Inside the tomb, the king would be laid to rest on a golden carpet. He would be dressed in his robes of state, and around him would be laid his provisions for after death— food and wine, together with his weapons. Animals would be sacrificed, roasted on fires lit within the tomb, and eaten by the mourners. Everyone would then have withdrawn, the doors would have been closed, and the entrance would have been filled up.

The dromos (entrance passage) of the Treasury of Atreus. The Treasury of Atreus is one of the most splendid examples of a tholos tomb.

the palace itself, with an open courtyard, anteroom, and state room (megaron), all surrounded by pantries and storerooms, together with the queen's apartments, which consisted of a smaller megaron, a boudoir, and a large bathroom with a terra-cotta bath.

Many clay tablets have been recovered from the palace at Pylos. When the palace was destroyed by fire around 1200 BCE, the fire may have actually preserved the tablets by baking them. The tablets generally record administrative matters, listing goods, palace personnel, and other details of housekeeping. By doing so, the tablets provide a snapshot of the palace administration just before the destruction. In addition, the tablets reveal much information about Mycenaean social life.

Mycenaean society

Despite its loose political organization, the Mycenaean world was surprisingly united in its social, religious, and linguistic aspects. Each region had its own king (*wanax*), who acted as its head. Under him was the *lawagetas* (people's leader), who was possibly an army commander. Then there were the *telestai*, who are thought to have been wealthy landowners. Freemen were referred to as *damos*. Each class had its own kind of landownership or tenancy.

Everything was controlled by the palace—the ownership and use of land, the labor employed, and the products of craftsmen. The tablets that have been recovered make it clear that most Mycenaeans were poor farmers who worked on land that was owned by the king. They grew crops such as barley and wheat and kept groves of olive trees to produce olive oil. They raised animals such as goats and sheep, which provided both meat and wool, and grew flax to make linen. Most of this produce had to be taken to the palace. It was then sold to

help support the royal family, priests, bureaucrats, and the army.

Another section of Mycenaean society included the skilled craftsmen. The most important of these were the bronzesmiths, who made the weapons for the army. There were also jewellers, potters, carpenters, and cabinetmakers, who carried out intricate inlay work. Large-scale textile manufacturing was carried out by spinners and weavers, most of whom were women. Many slaves were employed in Mycenaean society; most of them had been bought in slave markets in Anatolia.

The Mycenaeans were aggressive and warlike, and each king kept his own standing army, which he had to feed, clothe, and arm. The commanders of the

Tiryns, the ruins of which are seen here, was one of the most important Mycenaean cities.

MYCENAEAN RELIGION

There appear to have been many similarities between the Mycenaean and Minoan religions, but the two were not identical. Still, it seems that both civilizations did worship a mother goddess, whose divine son died at the death of the old year and was born again in the spring. Many Bronze Age paintings show people making offerings to this goddess.

Mycenaean tablets also mention the names of many gods, including Zeus, Athena, Artemis, Poseidon, and Dionysus, who were worshipped by later Greeks. At Pylos, Poseidon, the sea god who was the brother of Zeus, was an important deity who was depicted in the form of a horse. The name of Dionysus, the god of wine, is also found on Mycenaean tablets, which suggests that he too may have been worshipped at this time.

The Mycenaeans tended not to build temples to their gods. Instead, the people worshipped the gods at small shrines, some of which may have been located outdoors but most of which were found inside houses. Small terra-cotta idols in the shape of female figures have been recovered from Mycenae and other places, suggesting that the cult of the goddess was widespread. However, larger idols of both female and male figures have also been found, and it is possible that these idols represent the Greek gods.

These Mycenaean terra-cotta figures date to between 1400 and 1200 BCE. Archaeologists believe that the figures' flattened headdresses indicate that they depict goddesses.

Priests were an important part of Mycenaean society, and they would have carried out the religious rituals, which included sacrificing animals to the gods. The priests would also have conducted burials, and it is evident from the grave goods found in royal tombs from the period that the Mycenaeans believed that their kings would have a life after death.

army wore heavy armor made of bronze and leather helmets made fearsome with the addition of boar's tusks. The infantry wore tunics of leather and carried shields, swords, and daggers. Chariots, which usually carried two men and were drawn by two horses, played an important role in the army. Chariots were used both to lead charges in battle and to carry information back to headquarters.

The Mycenaeans came to dominate most of the Aegean area, subjugating Knossos on Crete and occupying other parts of the island. The influence of the Mycenaeans reached to all corners of their world—Asia Minor, Syria, Egypt, southern Italy, and the Mediterranean islands of Sicily, Cyprus, and Sardinia.

From the 1600s BCE onward, the Mycenaeans dominated sea trade in the Mediterranean. Trading posts were set up in southern Italy and Anatolia, and Mycenaean merchants traded goods such as cloth, pottery, grain, and oil with countries as far away as North Africa, Scandinavia, and the Middle East.

Decline and fall

Over the course of the 13th century BCE, the Mycenaeans carried out a significant amount of construction in their territory. Many new buildings were erected, and the fortresses of Tiryns, Mycenae, and Athens were expanded and reinforced. Even in Pylos, where there were no surrounding walls, the palace was modified to make it less open. Storerooms were enlarged and measures were taken to secure supplies of drinking water.

At the same time, in central Greece, a gigantic fortress was being erected near Gla, which is locat-ed on the edge of Lake Kopaïs in Boeotia. This fortress had walls 2 miles (3.2 km) long and covered a total area of 50 acres (202,343 m²). In comparison, Mycenae had walls slightly over 0.5 miles (0.8 km) long encircling an area of 7.5 acres (30,351 m²). The fortress at Gla was probably intended to be a central refuge for the entire surrounding area, at a time when Mycenaeans all over Greece were apparently feeling a threat of invasion.

This theory is borne out by clay tablets found at Pylos, which mention sending sentinels to the coast, drafting soldiers, and hiring rowers. One of the tablets refers to an unprecedented sacrifice of 13 golden vases and 10 people, obviously an attempt to secure the favor of the gods at a time of great emergency.

That the threat was not imaginary was proved by the widespread destruction that took place after 1250 BCE. This destruction has frequently been explained as the result of an invasion by the Dorians, a tribe from the Balkans and northern Greece. The Dorians are said to have annihilated the Mycenaean civilization, but this idea is flawed. There is no gap in the archaeological record that would correspond to the arrival of a huge group of newcomers. On the contrary, the overall impression is one of continuity after the destruction. Many of the former settlements were rebuilt, and the existing Mycenaean culture simply continued. However, the size of the population dropped dramatically, and society as a whole descended to a lower cultural plane.

So what caused the decline if it was not the Dorians? The whole eastern Mediterranean area was in ferment

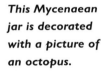

This Mycenaean jar is decorated with a picture of an octopus.

This cup, which was found in a Mycenaean tomb on the island of Rhodes, was made between 1350 and 1300 BCE.

at this time. The Hittites disappeared from Asia Minor while the Egyptians were battling with the Sea Peoples. It may be that these enemies of Egypt swept through the Mycenaean palaces, or there may have been civil war between the Mycenaean kingdoms. There may have been natural disasters, such as earthquakes, or the administrative and political systems may simply have collapsed as a result of famine or the cutting off of trade routes. Whatever the reason, the Mycenaean civilization disintegrated, and the so-called Dark Age dawned in Greece.

Troy

While the Mycenaean culture was dominant on the mainland of Greece, a city was flourishing in northwestern Anatolia. This city was Troy, the legendary adversary of Greece. As with Mycenae, much of what is known about Troy is the result of work carried out by the archaeologist Heinrich Schliemann.

The legendary city of Troy had fascinated Schliemann since boyhood, when his father had told him the stories of the *Iliad* and the *Odyssey* (see box, page 194) and Schliemann had come across an illustration of how the ancient city might

have looked. The city was supposed to have been encircled by a massive wall, punctuated by towers, and to have been the site of the Trojan War, the subject of the *Iliad*.

Troy did in fact exist more than 5,000 years ago. Bronze Age Troy was situated at the entrance to the Dardanelles, the route for ships passing between the Aegean Sea and the Black Sea. The city also occupied a crucial position on the land route between Europe and Asia. For these reasons, Troy became a prosperous mercantile city and a center of culture. In the third and second millennia BCE, it was the leading city of the region, with a royal house ruling over the surrounding farming villages. Troy continued to prosper until the middle of the 11th century BCE.

Schliemann's excavation

The true history of Troy was unknown in the mid-19th century CE, but several archaeologists, including Frank Calvert (1828–1908), were interested in discovering the site of ancient Troy (if it in fact existed). Calvert was an English amateur archaeologist working as a consular official in the Dardanelles area. He had read a book by Charles Maclaren (published in 1822) that suggested that a hill called Hissarlik on the Aegean coast of western Turkey might be the site of the city. Calvert's brother Frederick, who was also based in the area, bought a farm in 1847 that extended over 2,000 acres (8 km²) and took in part of Mount Hissarlik. Over the next few years, Frank made some exploratory excavations on his brother's land.

Since his retirement from the world of business around 1860, Heinrich Schliemann had been busy. He had studied archaeology, written a book on Troy, and traveled widely to visit sites of archaeological interest. In 1868, he met Frank Calvert in Turkey and learned of the preliminary excavations at Hissarlik. However, a full-scale excavation of the site would require considerable financing, which Calvert could not provide. Schliemann could, and he persuaded Calvert to let him take over the excavations on the Calvert half of the Hissarlik. Schliemann also obtained permission from the Turkish government to dig on the other half of the mound, as long as any discovered treasure was shared with the government.

Schliemann hired 70 local workmen and started digging in 1871. Very soon, he uncovered an ancient wall, built of immense boulders, just 15 feet (4.5 m) below the surface. Encouraged by this discovery, he then sank shafts and dug trenches into the hillside. To his amazement, he discovered the remains of not just one city, but nine cities, each built on the ruins of the last.

The treasure of Priam

Schliemann had certainly discovered an important archaeological site, but was it Troy? Although he called himself an archaeologist, Schliemann was primarily a treasure hunter. Later, at Mycenae, he would hope to unearth treasure belonging to Agamemnon. At the supposed site of Troy, he longed to find what he called "the treasure of Priam." Convinced that the Trojan War was grounded in historical fact, Schliemann felt sure that King Priam had hidden his treasures to save them from the Greeks.

Around noon on a day in June 1873, Schliemann spotted the gleam of gold at the base of a wall in the excavations. Schliemann and his wife, Sophia,

Neoptolemus is given the armor of his father Achilles by the Greek hero Odysseus. This vase illustration dates to around the eighth century BCE.

unearthed a cache of golden objects, including bracelets, earrings, diadems, and many gold rings. The Schliemanns hid the treasure and smuggled it off the site and, eventually, out of Turkey. When news of the find leaked out, the Turkish authorities were outraged at the deception. Schliemann had to pay a very heavy fine before he was allowed to continue excavating. Although Schliemann remained convinced he had discovered the treasure of King Priam, later research established that the golden horde dated from more than a thousand years before the time of the Trojan War.

Believing that the Troy of Homer would probably lie at almost the lowest level, Schliemann hired more men to dig down to that level. Unfortunately, since Schliemann understood nothing of the scientific method of archaeology, much valuable evidence was destroyed during the dig. Later archaeologists established that Homer's Troy lay at a much higher level.

The nine cities

The nine levels of Troy start with the first Troy, which was a small fortified citadel dating from around 3000 BCE. This citadel would have provided a safe shelter for the surrounding villagers when danger threatened. The second level was Troy II, dating from around 2600 BCE. The town was much larger and became wealthy by trading with the Mycenaeans of mainland Greece. The evidence points to Troy II being destroyed by fire, which was why Schliemann believed it was the Troy of

THE *ILIAD* AND THE *ODYSSEY*

The background to the story of the *Iliad* is the siege of Troy by a coalition of Greeks, called Achaeans in the poem. The reason for the war is that Helen, the beautiful wife of Menelaus, king of Sparta, has been abducted by Paris, a Trojan prince. When Menelaus discovers that his wife is gone, he and his brother Agamemnon, king of Mycenae, call upon the princes of Achaea to assist in punishing Troy and bringing Helen home. A fleet is prepared, and the warriors sail for Troy, where a drawn-out siege follows.

In the Greek camp outside Troy, a dispute arises between the Greek prince Achilles and the supreme commander, Agamemnon, who has abused his authority by taking a beautiful slave away from Achilles. Achilles, deeply insulted, refuses to continue fighting. Without Achilles, the Greeks prove to be weaker than the Trojans, and disaster threatens. Achilles finally agrees to allow his friend, Patroclus, to take part in the conflict, and Hector, the Trojan commander, kills Patroclus. The grieving Achilles feels compelled to avenge the death of his friend and in turn kills Hector, which heralds the beginning of the end for the Trojans.

The *Iliad* ends with the burial of Patroclus and the return of Hector's body to his father, King Priam.

The *Odyssey*, a sequel to the *Iliad*, deals with the difficult voyage home of one of the Greek princes, Odysseus of Ithaca. The tale opens with the stress that his prolonged absence has caused his household. Since no word has been heard from him for 10 years, Odysseus is assumed to be dead. Greedy suitors are ruining his property as they court his wife, Penelope.

Odysseus himself then relates his adventures to the king and queen of Scheria. Among other escapades, Odysseus tells them of his encounter with the man-eating giant Polyphemus and the temptations of the goddess Calypso, who offered Odysseus immortality.

The *Odyssey* ends with the return of Odysseus to the island of Ithaca, where the hero discovers what has been going on in his absence. He kills the suitors who have been besieging his supposed widow and is reunited with his wife, son, and aged father.

This Roman mosaic depicts Odysseus being tempted by the sirens.

Homer. The three succeeding Troys were each larger than the one before.

Troy VI was heavily influenced by the Mycenaeans and attracted many new settlers. It was destroyed around 1300 BCE, to be succeeded by what is called Troy VIIa. Most archaeologists now believe that this is the Homeric Troy. Fragments of pottery found at this level indicate that the city dates from the mid-13th century BCE. Some human remains, one of which is a human skeleton showing injuries to the head and a broken jawbone, have been found in the streets, which suggests the city was destroyed by war. There is also evidence that Troy VIIa was put to the torch. The next city, Troy VIIb, also seems to have been destroyed by fire. Historians believe this destruction happened around 1050 BCE.

The fall of Troy

After the destruction of Troy VIIb, the city seems to have been abandoned for several centuries, but at the start of the seventh century BCE, the site was reoccupied by Greeks and became known as Ilium. Around 85 BCE, this city was attacked and taken by the Romans, who then built Troy IX, which became an important trading city until it was eclipsed by Constantinople in the fourth century CE. Around 400 CE, the site was finally abandoned and gradually disappeared under the mound of Hissarlik, until the cities were finally rediscovered by Schliemann.

Schliemann died in 1890, and the work at Hissarlik was carried on by his assistant, Wilhelm Dorpfeld, who made further excavations in 1893 and 1894. After that point, nothing more was done until the 1930s, when the American archaeologist Carl Blegen (1887–1971) carried out careful excavations over a seven-year period, from 1932 to 1938. He took many photographs and was instrumental in establishing much of the chronology of the city. In particular, it was Blegen who established that the Troy of Homeric legend was almost certainly Troy VIIa.

See also:

Bronze Age Greece (volume 2, page 162) •
The Minoans (volume 2, page 170)

THE PHOENICIANS

The Phoenicians were a seafaring people who built up a vast trading network around the Mediterranean Sea in the third and second millenniums BCE. They were also responsible for creating one of the world's earliest alphabets.

By the beginning of the first millennium BCE, the Phoenicians were renowned as intrepid seafarers and astute traders throughout the Mediterranean area. From their base on the shores of the eastern Mediterranean, they set up trading posts throughout the region, becoming the carriers of the Mediterranean world. They also provided a vital link to the caravans that brought exotic merchandise from the east.

No one is sure where the Phoenicians originally came from, but they were probably settled in what is now Syria, Lebanon, and Israel by around 3000 BCE. In their own language, they called themselves Canaanites, which suggests they may have been descended from the original inhabitants of the land of Canaan (present-day Palestine). In the Semitic language, however, *Canaan* also means "the land of purple," so the name may be unconnected to their geographical origins and refer merely to the purple dye for which the Phoenicians were famous.

The Phoenicians occupied a narrow strip of land around 260 miles (418 km) northeast of Egypt that consisted of the coastal area of today's Lebanon, together with parts of modern Israel and Syria. Bordered by the Lebanon Mountains to the east, this fertile area was around 200 miles (321 km) long and around 30 miles (48 km) wide. From this small base, the Phoenicians eventually dominated trade throughout the Mediterranean region.

Early history

Between 3000 and 2000 BCE, the Phoenicians built several cities, including Ugarit and Byblos. By around 2600 BCE, the Phoenicians were trading with merchants in Egypt. There is a record of an Egyptian expedition to the Phoenician port of Byblos around this time to buy 40 shiploads of cedar wood.

By 1500 BCE, the Phoenician ports had become thriving trading centers, but the second half of the millennium was to see the Phoenicians lose their independence to a succession of foreign invaders, including the Egyptians, the Hittites, and the Mycenaeans. Around 1100 BCE, however, the Phoenicians were able to throw off foreign domination and to emerge as the dominant sea power of the Mediterranean region.

Phoenicia wielded an influence far beyond its size. Its great cities of Arvad, Byblos, Ugarit, Berytus, Sidon, and Tyre were hubs of international trade. These cities set up trading stations and colonies in Sicily and Cyprus, and as far away as Gades (present-day Cadiz) in Spain. In 814 BCE, the city of Tyre established a colony called Carthage on the north coast of Africa. Carthage would become the most powerful Phoenician city of all.

Independent kingdoms

Phoenicia was not one united kingdom; it operated as a loose confederation of city-states. Each city had its own king, who came from a royal family that claimed divine descent, which meant that the king could only be chosen from that family. The king ruled with the help of a council of elders chosen from the most powerful merchant families. These elders appointed magistrates who were entrusted with the administration of daily government.

The greatest of the city-states was Tyre (meaning "rock"), which was actually made up of two distinct parts—an

This terra-cotta mask was made by Phoenician craftsmen around the seventh century BCE.

197

offshore island and a town on the nearby mainland. The island had two harbors, along with a number of closely packed houses, some of which were several stories high, built on the rocks. Into these houses was crammed a teaming population of timber merchants, shipbuilders, sailors, weavers, and cloth dyers.

Trading in timber

One of Phoenicia's most valuable resources was timber. The region's mountains were covered in forests of Lebanon cedars, trees that were valuable for the exceptionally hard timber they yielded. The Phoenicians built their own ships out of this material but also exported a great deal, particularly to Egypt, which had no trees of its own apart from palm trees.

The rot-resistant qualities of the cedar wood made it especially valuable for shipbuilding, and ancient historical records show that the Egyptian pharaohs used Phoenician wood for both their private boats and their holy ships. Around 950 BCE, King Solomon of Israel imported Lebanon cedar to use as the beams for his temple in Jerusalem. He also recruited Phoenician carpenters and construction workers to handle the project because, according to the Bible, nobody could work with wood as well as the Sidonians, as the Israelites called the Phoenicians.

Another important export was cloth, particularly the purple-dyed cloth used by royalty (see box, page 202), while glassworkers made highly prized glass vessels from the fine white sand found on Phoenicia's shores (see box, page 200). Phoenician craftsmen also worked with imported metals and other raw materials to produce finely wrought jewelry and tools for export. Delicate, decorative panels were carved from African ivory and used to embellish furniture produced by Phoenician carpenters.

Lords of the sea

In the early part of the first millennium BCE, the Phoenicians were the preeminent sailors in the Mediterranean region. While this status was partly due to their seamanship, the quality of their ships was also an important factor. Phoenician ships had a wide, flat hull to hold plenty of cargo, while a double deck offered space for two rows of oarsmen. With a square sail on a single mast, these ships were fast and highly maneuverable. They enabled the Phoenicians to criss-cross the Mediterranean and even venture into the Atlantic and Indian oceans.

The Phoenicians were first and foremost traders. As well as importing goods and exporting their own raw materials and products, the Phoenicians acted as

THE PHOENICIAN WORLD

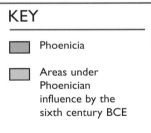

KEY

| | Phoenicia |
| | Areas under Phoenician influence by the sixth century BCE |

wholesalers, retailers, and transporters of goods. Phoenicia was ideally situated for trade, lying between the prosperous Egyptians to the south and the Hittites to the northwest and on the main caravan routes that brought goods from Mesopotamia and the east to the Mediterranean and northern Africa. Although they were known primarily as seafaring merchants, the Phoenicians did not conduct their trade exclusively by sea; they carried goods by land as far as Babylon in present-day Iraq.

The Phoenicians established good relations with the major powers of the eastern Mediterranean. In 950 BCE, Israel's King Solomon entered into a trade agreement with King Hiram of Tyre to do business with the people living on the coast of the Red Sea. This arrangement probably extended to the people of western Arabia and beyond—the land of Ophir in the Bible. The pharaohs of Egypt employed Phoenicians to help build and sail fleets, and to equip expeditions. The Egyptians even allowed Phoenicia to establish a trading post at Memphis, in the heart of commercial Egypt.

Carthage and other colonies

At a great many strategic points along the Mediterranean coastline, the Phoenicians owned warehouses and trading posts. Over the years, some of these posts developed into large colonies and cities, the most famous of which is Carthage (in present-day Tunisia).

Carthage was founded in 814 BCE by a group of discontented or exiled citizens of Tyre, who had been forced to leave their country for political reasons. They sailed to the African coast and landed near Utica, one of Tyre's colonies. At that landing spot, they founded a new colony called Qart-hadasht (meaning "new city"), later known as Carchédon to the Greeks and Carthage to the Romans. There are several mythical versions of the story about the founding of this city. The most famous version is in Virgil's *Aeneid*, where the city is founded by Queen Dido, a fugitive from Tyre who becomes the lover of the Trojan hero Aeneas.

Carthage was located on a large bay and enjoyed a natural harbor—one of the best in the Mediterranean. The site could be easily defended and was perfectly situated for overseas trade. In the centuries following its foundation, Carthage grew into a rich and powerful city, trading in goods and materials such as textiles, pottery, and silver mined in Africa and Spain. Carthage continued to flourish until it was eventually destroyed by Roman forces in 146 BCE.

The Phoenicians had a knack for finding strategic places. They founded a colony at Massilia (present-day Marseilles) long before the Greeks. They also founded a number of settlements in Spain; Phoenician colonies at Gades and present-day Barcelona, Málaga, and Algeciras were important because of Spain's abundance of copper and silver.

Gades was the last stop before Phoenician ships sailed out into the Atlantic on what was one of their longest and most demanding voyages—a trading expedition to a place that the Phoenicians called the Tin Islands. This destination was actually the British Isles, where tin was mined in the extreme southwest (present-day Cornwall). The Phoenicians mixed the tin with copper to make bronze.

Navigation and exploration

Voyages beyond the confines of the Mediterranean were only possible because of the Phoenicians' superior seamanship and navigating abilities. On every voyage, the Phoenician captains made careful observation of shores, distances, landmarks, currents, and wind direction. By doing so, they built up a wealth of precise navigational knowledge. They are also believed to have been the first sailors to use the Pole Star (Polaris) as an aid to navigation. Because of the lucrative nature of their business,

PHOENICIAN GLASSWARE

The white sand that lined the shores of Phoenicia was the source of silica, which, with wood ash, was an essential ingredient for the transparent glass that provided the Phoenicians with an important export. The Phoenician glassworkers were highly skilled in glassmaking and in producing beautifully decorated glassware. Although the Phoenicians may have invented glassblowing, most of their glassware was produced by a simpler technique called the sand-core method.

For this technique, the craftsman made a mold of sand in the required shape and then poured molten glass over the mold. When the glass coating had cooled and set, the sand was emptied out, leaving a hollow glass vessel. Patterns of different colored glass were then dripped on to the vessel, which was then rolled on a flat surface to set the pattern before the glass cooled. The result would be an elegant piece of highly decorative glassware that was prized throughout the Mediterranean region.

This stone relief from the palace of the Assyrian king Sargon II depicts wood being unloaded from Phoenician ships. The relief dates to the eighth century BCE.

the Phoenicians guarded the secrets of their routes carefully, so no one else would be able to profit by them.

The Phoenicians' reputation as daring seafarers ensured that they were often hired by other nations to carry out adventurous voyages. Around 600 BCE, the Egyptian pharaoh Necho commissioned a Phoenician expedition to explore the coast of Africa. The ships sailed out through the Red Sea and returned to the Mediterranean several years later through the Strait of Gibraltar. In the fifth century BCE, the Greek historian Herodotus wrote the following account of the expedition: "They sailed south along the coast. In winter, the fleet looked for a safe haven where they sowed grain. After the harvest, the Phoenician ships moved on with fresh provisions on board. This way, the voyage around Africa took three years."

When they returned home, the Phoenician sailors claimed that they had seen the sun to the north. While this was unbelievable to their contemporaries, the report lends credence to the story that the Phoenicians passed the equator. In the Northern Hemisphere, the midday sun appears to be slightly to the south, because Earth is tilted on its axis. The reverse is true in the Southern Hemisphere—the sun appears to be to the north at midday. So, it seems likely that the Phoenicians did indeed sail completely around Africa.

The voyage of Hanno

One of the most famous Phoenician voyages took place in the late fifth century BCE, when a large expedition set out from Carthage with the explorer Hanno at its head. The purpose of the expedition was to found colonies along

PURPLE CLOTH

The Phoenicians were famous for their purple cloth, which came mainly from the city of Tyre. The color of the cloth was produced with the help of a purple dye obtained from the murex snail, a type of sea snail. These molluscs abounded in the sea around Tyre, and they were harvested by the thousands to make the dye. The process began when the shells were cracked open to remove the sea creature from inside. The soft bodies were then left to rot, producing a hideous stench for which Tyre was notorious. Once they had rotted, the bodies were pressed to extract a yellow liquid. When this liquid was boiled, it turned a dark purple.

Because only a tiny drop of liquid was yielded by each snail, an enormous number of molluscs were needed to produce a reasonable amount of the dye, making it a very expensive product. The Phoenician cloth dyers were skilled in using the liquid to dye cloth in colors varying from pale pink to dark purple. The purple cloth was much in demand because it was the color from which royal robes were made.

the Atlantic coast of Morocco. Hanno was provided with an enormous fleet and a vast number of colonists to carry out this task (see box, page 205).

The log of Hanno's voyage is unusual in that it has survived. The fact that so few Phoenician logs have come to light may be because they were kept secret and few copies or translations were ever made. The Phoenicians were anxious to guard their navigational secrets because those secrets were the basis of Phoenician prosperity. The Phoenicians maintained their secrets about trade in the Atlantic so successfully that the Greeks and Romans never discovered who the trading partners were.

One story that has survived relates how a Phoenician ship in the Atlantic deliberately changed course and ran aground when it realized that a Roman ship was spying on it. The Roman vessel followed its target onto the rocks and was wrecked as well. All hands were lost—only the Phoenician captain survived. When the captain finally returned home, he was rewarded with a large sum of money for eluding the attentions of the Romans and received full compensation for his lost cargo.

Despite the fact that the Phoenicians guarded their navigational secrets zealously, some of their knowledge did become known to the Greeks. Greek sailors from the island of Rhodes compiled a navigational manual called *The Captain of the Mediterranean*, which contained everything they knew about trade routes, winds, and ocean currents. It described the most favorable times for crossing the sea and gave advice on avoiding bad weather, rounding the ocean capes, and benefiting from the wind. This manual compiled by the Greeks remained until the 19th century CE an indispensable guide for vessels navigating the Mediterranean.

Methods of trade

The Phoenicians developed their own ingenious methods for trading with the indigenous peoples they encountered on their voyages to the Atlantic seaboard of Africa. According to Herodotus, the Carthaginians would sail to the west coast of Africa each year at the same time. They would deposit the goods they wanted to trade on a beach and then return to their ships. The local inhabitants would emerge from the jungle and place as much gold next to the merchandise as they saw fit. The Phoenicians would then return and inspect the gold, to determine whether the amount was sufficient. If it was not, they would return to their ships without touching anything. The Africans would then add more gold to the pile. This procedure might be repeated several times before the parties came to an agreement. Only when the

Phoenicians deemed the pile of gold to be sufficient would they take it and embark, leaving the local inhabitants to take the goods.

The alphabet

Despite their great exploits as seafarers, the most important legacy that the Phoenicians left is their alphabet. The earliest writing systems consisted of pictographs (hieroglyphs), simple pictures that represented objects or ideas. The beginning of a true alphabet occurs when a pictograph comes to represent part of the sound of a word, rather than the idea behind it.

The Phoenician settlements on the eastern shore of the Mediterranean were surrounded by four major cultures, each of which had its own script. To the north were the Hittites, who used a hieroglyphic script of such complexity that it

The remains of the forum at Carthage. Founded by exiles from Tyre, Carthage rose to become one of the western Mediterranean's most powerful city-states.

has still not been completely deciphered. To the east, the Mesopotamians had a cuneiform script that used symbols for the different syllables of a word. The Cretans and Mycenaeans to the west had two systems of writing (called Linear A and Linear B), as well as symbols to represent syllables. To the south, the Egyptians originally used hieroglyphs, but in the second millennium BCE, a script called the sacerdotal was developed. This script drew the hieroglyphs in an abbreviated form, in much the same way that a modern stenographer writes the alphabet in short form. The sacerdotal script bore some similarity to an alphabetical script but contained as many symbols as the hieroglyphic script. All of these writing systems used hundreds of different symbols and could not be called an alphabet in the modern sense of the word.

The first true alphabet, called North Semitic, originated on the eastern Mediterranean shore between 1700 and 1500 BCE and consisted of signs representing consonants, as do today's related Hebrew and Arabic variants. Other branches, including the Phoenician, developed from the original Semitic alphabet in the 11th century BCE.

The Phoenician script came to light in 1876, when a Syrian farmer turned up copper beakers bearing inscriptions from the time of King Hiram of Tyre, who ruled around 950 BCE. The farmer broke the beakers to sell the metal, and only a few fragments with inscriptions were recovered. The writing on those fragments is the known Semitic script and reads from right to left.

More finds were made in 1922, when a number of royal tombs were excavated

This colonnade is found in Tyre, which was one of the richest and most powerful of the Phoenician city-states. It was located in present-day Lebanon.

HANNO'S VOYAGE

The expedition of the Carthaginian explorer Hanno is well documented in the voyage's log, which has been preserved. The log records that Hanno "departed with 60 ships, each with 50 rowers. On board were men, women, and children, totalling 30,000."

Two days after sailing past the Strait of Gibraltar, the expedition made landfall and founded a city called Thymiaterion. "From there to Cape Libya," continues the log, "stretched a vast, tree-covered plain. There we built a temple for Poseidon, the god of the sea, and then sailed on to the south. We reached a lake where there were elephants and other wild animals. After another day of travel we founded new colonies and reached the river Lixos. A tribe of Berber shepherds lived on the banks of this river with their flocks; we befriended them and rested for a few days." They then sailed on for three more days, reaching a bay where they founded another colony. They believed this place to be as far to the west of the Strait of Gibraltar as Carthage was to the east. Eventually, the expedition reached a large river up which they sailed, coming to a lake on the banks of which rose great mountains. "On their slopes," records the log, "roamed wild people dressed in animal skins who pelted us with stones. From there we came to another wide river with many crocodiles and hippopotamuses." Back at the coast, they continued to sail south, noting that the land was inhabited by "Ethiopians" (by which they meant black Africans). After three weeks' sailing, they came to a gulf where many "wild people" lived. "Their bodies were completely covered with hair," notes the log, "and our interpreters called them gorillas. We tried to catch one but we did not succeed in catching a male because they climbed into trees and defended themselves with stones. We did catch three females, but because they bit everyone, we had to kill them. After we had skinned them, we took their hides back to the city of Carthage."

Although these hairy "people" were described as gorillas, it seems probable that they were actually chimpanzees, since gorillas would not have been so easy to catch. After this encounter, Hanno decided that the expedition was running out of provisions, and they turned back. It is not known quite how far south Hanno sailed, but it seems probable that the expedition traveled as far as Sierra Leone.

This stone relief depicts a Phoenician merchant vessel. The Phoenicians' considerable seafaring skills enabled them to make great voyages of discovery, such as that made by the explorer Hanno.

RELIGION AND SACRIFICE

The Phoenicians worshipped a large number of gods and goddesses, and each of the city-states had its own patron deity. For example, the citizens of Tyre worshipped a god called Melqart, who was a sun god. As might be expected from a god worshipped by seafarers, Melqart was also seen as a protector of navigators. When traders from Tyre set up a new colony, they made sacrifices to Melqart and would wait for a positive sign from the god before they settled. One of the first buildings to be constructed would be a temple to the god.

Melqart's consort was the fertility goddess Astarte, who was known by various names throughout the Mediterranean, including Astoret, Asherah, and Ashratu. She was closely linked to the Babylonian goddess Ishtar and the Egyptian goddess Isis. Astarte's equivalent in Carthage was Tanit. Although Tanit was the wife of the god Baal Hammon, she seems to have been seen as the more important deity. Like Astarte, Tanit was a fertility goddess.

Some historians believe that the Phoenicians practiced some form of child sacrifice. According to Greek writers such as Diodorus Siculus (first century BCE), children would be burned in sacred fires in front of their parents. Diodorus wrote that hundreds of children were sacrificed in Carthage when the city was besieged by Greek Sicilian forces in 310 BCE. Other historians dispute the view. They argue that the burnt remains of children's bones found in sacred hearths came from children who had died naturally and point out that most of the stories of child sacrifice come from cultures that were enemies of the Phoenicians.

This gold necklace was made by Phoenician craftsmen around the fifth century BCE.

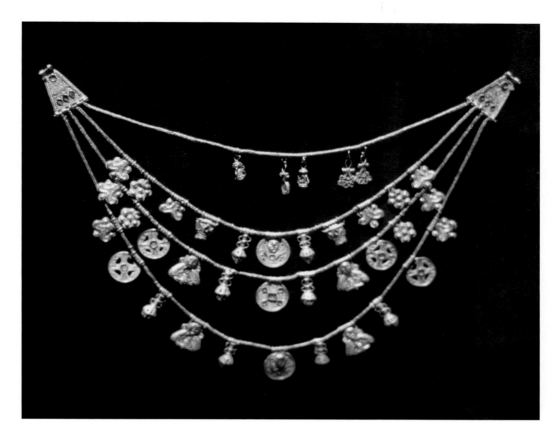

The ruins of the Hall of the Ambassador at Ugarit. Ugarit was one of the wealthiest Phoenician cities.

in Byblos. The stone coffin of King Ahiram, who ruled in the early 10th century BCE, contained an elaborate text in the linear Phoenician alphabet.

The Greeks adopted the Phoenician alphabet in the eighth century BCE, making only minor changes to the shape of the letters. The Greeks expanded the 22 Phoenician consonants to 24 and made some symbols serve as vowels. After around 500 BCE, the Greeks started writing from left to right.

The Greek alphabet was adopted and adapted throughout the Mediterranean world. When it passed to the Romans, they spread it via Latin throughout the Roman Empire. The Greek alphabet was therefore destined to become the basis of all Western alphabets.

Foreign domination again

In 842 BCE, most of the Phoenician cities on the eastern Mediterranean coast lost their independence when they became absorbed into the Assyrian Empire during the campaigns of conquest of the Assyrian king Shalmaneser III. From this point onward, the Phoenicians came under the control of a succession of foreign powers.

Phoenicia remained part of the Assyrian Empire until the late seventh century BCE and then came under the control of the Babylonians. The region fell to the Persian forces of Cyrus the Great in 539 BCE. Under Persian rule, the cities enjoyed some freedoms and were able to prosper again commercially, but Phoenicia was not to survive. In 330 BCE, the region was conquered by the Macedonian general Alexander the Great. Finally, in 64 BCE, Phoenicia became part of the Roman Empire and lost all separate identity.

See also:

The Israelites (volume 2, page 222) • The Punic Wars (volume 4, page 464)

THE ASSYRIANS

c. 2000 BCE
Distinct Assyrian culture emerges in northern Mesopotamia.

c. 1760 BCE
Old Empire comes to end after Ashur conquered by Babylonians.

c. 1250 BCE
Shalmaneser I conquers Mitanni Empire to greatly expand area controlled by Assyrians.

c. 883 BCE
Ashurnasirpal II begins campaigns of imperial expansion, expanding Assyrian territory; he also restores city of Nimrud.

c. 729 BCE
Tiglath-pileser III unites Assyria and Babylonia under one rule.

c. 612 BCE
Nineveh falls to Babylonians; Assyrian Empire comes to end three years later.

Known for their ruthlessness in subjugating their enemies, the Assyrians dominated large sections of western Asia for much of the second and first millenniums BCE. A visual record of their conquests can be found at their ancient capital of Nimrud.

Assyria was one of the earliest empires to be established in western Asia. The core of the Assyrian heartland lay to the north of Babylonia, between the Tigris River to the west and the Zagros Mountains to the east. The discovery of two Neanderthal skulls in the area showed that the area has been inhabited since Paleolithic times. There is also evidence that early farmers settled in this fertile area around the ninth millennium BCE. They grew wheat and barley, kept domesticated animals, and built houses of clay. They are also known to have baked bread in clay ovens, spun thread using hand spindles, woven cloth, and made tools, ornaments, and seals out of stone.

During the third millennium BCE, the region came under the influence of the Akkadian civilization, and the inhabitants adopted the Akkadian language and cuneiform script. When the southern empires of Sumer and Akkad collapsed around 2000 BCE, a distinct Assyrian culture began to emerge. However, nothing was known of this culture until the 19th century CE, when two outstanding archaeologists—Paul Emile Botta and Austen Henry Layard—excavated the cities of Nineveh, Nimrud, and Dur Sharrukin (Khorsabad). The spectacular finds that Botta and Layard made unravelled the story of one of the great lost civilizations of western Asia.

Historians usually divide the history of the Assyrian Empire into three periods: the Old Empire (c. 2000–1760 BCE), the Middle Empire (c. 1363–1000 BCE), and the New Empire (c. 1000–612 BCE). During the period of the Old Empire, the Assyrians established a number of city-states, including Ashur, Nineveh, and Arbela. Each city consisted of a palace, temples, and a maze of houses, all enclosed within a city wall. Ashur, named after the god of the same name, was the center of a remarkable trading network. A merchant colony was set up in the city of Kanesh in Anatolia, and pottery vessels full of cuneiform texts discovered there give a picture of a flourishing trade in copper and textiles, carried by caravans of donkeys. This lucrative enterprise was controlled by just 10 or 15 Assyrian families, and their burial sites discovered in Ashur attest to their great wealth.

The rule of Shamshi-Adad I

From around 1813 BCE, Assyria came under the rule of Shamshi-Adad I (ruled c. 1813–1781 BCE), a prince of an Amorite dynasty. He had imperialist

These remains of a ziggurat are located at Nimrud. The city reached the height of its wealth in the ninth century BCE, hundreds of years after it was founded.

ambitions and conquered an area that extended from Assyria in the east to Mari on the Euphrates River in the west and Babylonia in the south. Ruling from Ashur, Shamshi-Adad established what was probably the first centrally organized empire of the ancient Middle East. At the death of Shamshi-Adad, his son Ishme-Dagan I succeeded to the throne. During Ishme-Dagan's reign, King Hammurabi of Babylonia captured Ashur, bringing the Assyrian Old Empire to an end. Assyria became part of the Babylonian Empire around 1760 BCE.

Toward the end of the third millennium BCE, a new population group arrived in Mesopotamia. The Hurrians founded large colonies on the upper reaches of the Euphrates and Tigris rivers. These colonies were the forerunners of the Mitanni Empire. By around 1500 BCE, the Hurrian Mitanni kingdom had come to dominate northern Mesopotamia. The kingdom subjugated Assyria, maintaining regional control for the next century, while the Hittites were establishing their rival empire to the north. Around 1363 BCE, while the Mitanni were preoccupied with the Hittites, the Assyrian king Ashur-uballit I successfully attacked the Mitanni and won back Assyrian freedom. This marked the beginning of the Middle Empire.

The Middle Empire

As head of the newly independent Assyria, Ashur-uballit called himself the "Great King" and considered himself the equal of the king of Egypt. Ashur-uballit named Assyria the "Land of Ashur," and he and his successors set about restoring the might of the empire.

After Ashur-uballit's death in 1328 BCE, a drawn-out war with Babylonia ensued. Successive Assyrian kings also led campaigns to the east and north to suppress hostile tribes that threatened the borders. To the west, the Assyrian army

reached the Euphrates River around 1300 BCE, under the leadership of Adad-nirari I (ruled c. 1305–1274 BCE). In 1250 BCE, Adad-nirari's son King Shalmaneser I succeeded in annexing the Mitanni Empire, thereby greatly extending his own empire.

Shalmaneser's son Tukulti-Ninurta I (ruled c. 1233–1197 BCE) was a gifted sovereign under whom Assyria achieved unprecedented power. He took on the might of Babylonia, defeated its army, sacked the city of Babylon, and plundered its temples. He was the first king to carry out large-scale deportations to ensure peace in the empire, but his ruthless methods made him so unpopular that eventually his sons instigated a rebellion in which he was killed.

The coming of the Sea Peoples

Around 1200 BCE, a period of great unrest began in the Mesopotamian region. A group of invaders known to the Egyptians as the Sea Peoples defeated the Hittites in Anatolia, while the Aramaeans made incursions into Mesopotamia. The Assyrian king Tiglath-pileser I (ruled c. 1114–1076 BCE) reacted strongly to this threat, raiding and razing Aramaean villages and seizing or massacring anyone who did not flee. Nevertheless, the Aramaeans continued their onslaughts. By around 1000 BCE, they were firmly entrenched in the west and seemed poised to take over the entire Assyrian kingdom. Assyria, and indeed the whole region, was entering a dark age, perhaps caused, and certainly made worse, by drought and famine.

During the Middle Empire period, the Assyrian state had developed into a strong military power. Constant battles to protect the Assyrian borders had honed an efficient army (see box, page 214), which was greatly strengthened by the introduction of the horse-drawn chariot. The wealth of the state depended on

THE GROWTH OF THE ASSYRIAN EMPIRE

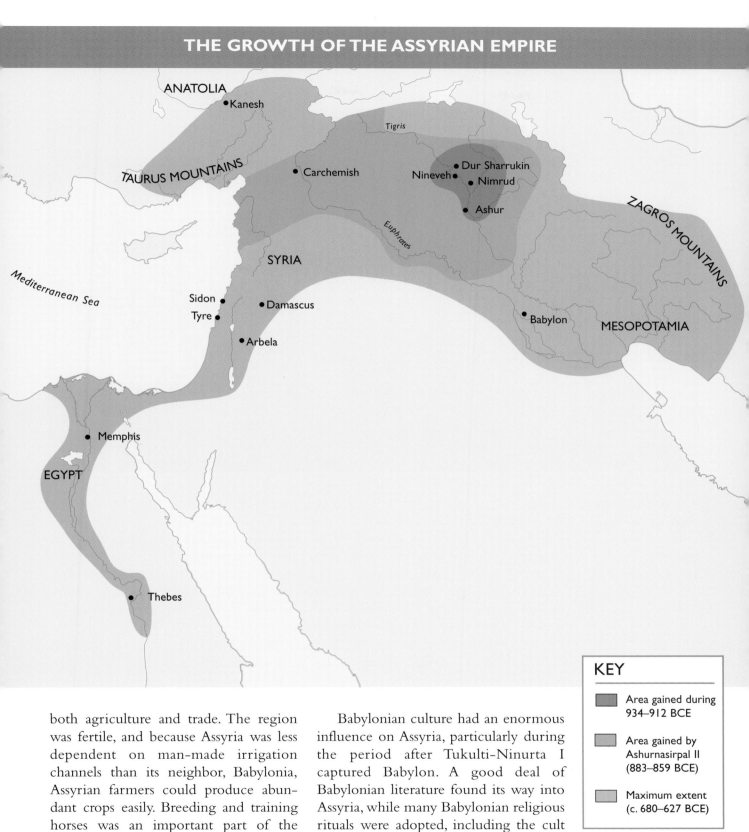

ANATOLIA
• Kanesh

TAURUS MOUNTAINS

Tigris

Carchemish

Nineveh • • Dur Sharrukin
• Nimrud

• Ashur

ZAGROS MOUNTAINS

Euphrates

SYRIA

Mediterranean Sea

Sidon •
Tyre •
• Damascus

• Arbela

• Babylon   MESOPOTAMIA

• Memphis

EGYPT

• Thebes

KEY

Area gained during 934–912 BCE

Area gained by Ashurnasirpal II (883–859 BCE)

Maximum extent (c. 680–627 BCE)

both agriculture and trade. The region was fertile, and because Assyria was less dependent on man-made irrigation channels than its neighbor, Babylonia, Assyrian farmers could produce abundant crops easily. Breeding and training horses was an important part of the economy, and Assyrian horses were famous throughout the Middle East.

Babylonian culture had an enormous influence on Assyria, particularly during the period after Tukulti-Ninurta I captured Babylon. A good deal of Babylonian literature found its way into Assyria, while many Babylonian religious rituals were adopted, including the cult of the god Marduk. The Assyrians took over the Babylonian calendar and

Assyrian soldiers are depicted defending a fortress in this relief from the eighth century BCE.

changed their system of weights and measures to that of the Babylonians. The Babylonian influence can also be seen in Assyrian art and architecture.

Many of the tablets discovered by archaeologists have provided a comprehensive picture of the legal system that was in place in the Middle Empire. Punishments for infractions of the law were extremely severe, ranging from beatings to mutilation and death. Women had very few rights. A husband could divorce his wife at will, and if she committed adultery, he could maim her or even kill her. Women led very restricted lives and had to wear veils whenever they went out in public.

The New Empire

By around 900 BCE, the Hittite Empire had disappeared. Mesopotamia and Syria were suffering under attacks from the Aramaean tribes, whose centers of power included southern Babylonia and the area surrounding Damascus. Assyria, which was increasingly on the defensive, had been forced back from the border formed by the Euphrates River in the west.

Around the beginning of the ninth century BCE, things began to change. Two kings—Adad-nirari II (ruled c. 911–891 BCE) and Tukulti-Ninurta II (ruled c. 890–884 BCE)—succeeded in winning back territory from the Aramaeans and regaining the banks of the Euphrates River. Their successes marked a turning point in Assyrian fortunes. Ashurnasirpal II, the son of Tukulti-Ninurta II, ruled from 883 to 859 BCE and continued his father's policy of reconquest, isolating the Aramaean city-states one by one and destroying them. He was a brilliant and ruthless general, and his own accounts of his campaigns testify to their terrifying cruelty. It was his custom to impale his defeated enemies on stakes, flay them alive, or behead them. He also deported the local citizenry en masse, thereby robbing the conquered region of its indigenous people and creating a subjugated population throughout the empire.

Military tactics

Ashurnasirpal's campaigns were helped by the fact that he made substantial use of units of cavalry, in addition to his war chariots and infantry. He also used mobile battering rams to break down the walls of cities under siege. Once he had taken a city, he made sure that Assyrian officials quickly took over its administration, thereby ensuring that the new conquest was incorporated into the Assyrian Empire smoothly and efficiently without any loss of time.

By attacking the regions on Assyria's immediate borders, Ashurnasirpal was able to extend his rule as far as the Mediterranean Sea. He annexed Phoenician coastal cities and small states on the Mediterranean coast and forced them to pay annual tribute to Assyria. It was not advisable to resist the Assyrian army; no one was spared if a city had to be taken by force.

The following is Ashurnasirpal's own account of the taking of the fortress of Hulai: "I surrounded the city with the main force of my troops. After a wild battle in the field, I took it. I slew 600 of his warriors with my weapons; 3,000 prisoners I burned in a great fire; I did not take a single hostage.... I stacked the bodies like towers; the young men and girls I burned alive. I skinned the king of Hulai alive and hung his skin on the city walls. I demolished and burned the city."

LAYARD'S DISCOVERIES

Much of the existing knowledge about the Assyrians is the result of the work of British archaeologist Austen Henry Layard (1817–1894). Layard began excavating the ancient Assyrian city of Nimrud in 1845. At the time, he was unaware that he had uncovered the palace and capital of Ashurnasirpal II. However, as Layard and his team worked on, they discovered a number of magnificent artifacts that revealed much about the life of the Assyrian king who ruled in the ninth century BCE.

Among the treasures found at Nimrud was a statue of Ashurnasirpal himself, which had once stood in the temple of the goddess Ishtar. There were a number of huge stone sphinxes, which had guarded the palace. There were also relief sculptures depicting scenes from royal life. One object that contained a number of such reliefs was the Black Obelisk, a stele that stood nearly 7 feet (2.1 m) tall. The stele, which was crowned by three steps in the shape of a ziggurat, showed scenes of foreign kings paying tribute to Shalmaneser III, Ashurnasirpal's son and successor. Assyrian kings often collected animals as trophies, and the illustrations on the obelisk show a number of exotic beasts, including an elephant and a rhinoceros, being brought to the king.

Cultural impact

Despite the many atrocities that he committed, Ashurnasirpal proved to be a positive cultural force. He commissioned architects, sculptors, and artists to build or enlarge several temples and palaces, and the resulting works exhibited a quality never before achieved. He restored the city of Nimrud (ancient Calah), making it his capital in place of Ashur. This was a mammoth project. The city wall itself needed around 70 million bricks of sun-dried clay to enclose an area of around 864 acres (350 ha). Inside this wall was built a magnificent palace, which covered an area of 269,000 square feet (25,000 m²).

The palace, based on a modified version of an ancient pattern, had two com-

THE ASSYRIAN ARMY

During the New Empire, the Assyrian army developed from a part-time amateur force that was conscripted for plundering raids to a highly professional standing army that was one of the most efficient and deadly fighting forces ever known. Up until the ninth century BCE, the army consisted mainly of peasants and farmers who were forced to join the king on his annual campaigns. In theory, all men had to do military duty, but many wealthy Assyrians managed to evade service by providing slaves instead. These conscripts, led by a core of professional soldiers, consisted mostly of light infantrymen armed with bows and arrows, slings, pikes, spears, battle-axes, and swords. Of these light infantrymen, the archers were the most important. Troops in the heavy infantry were also equipped with armor.

By the ninth century BCE, a standing army had been formed. The commander in chief was the king, who often led campaigns in person. The bulk of the army consisted of foreign contingents of foot soldiers conscripted from various subjugated lands and led by Assyrian officers. The army was divided into units of varying size. The company, which was the basic unit, consisted of 50 men under the command of a captain.

The elite of the army were the charioteers. Each chariot carried a driver, an archer, and usually one or two shield bearers to protect the driver and archer. The chariots were backed up by cavalry, which rode bareback and operated in pairs. One cavalryman wielded a short bow, while his partner carried a shield to protect him.

The marching army was followed by engineers who would build bridges and other structures. Engineers were also in charge of battering rams, siege towers, and other devices, such as scaling ladders, that were used in siege warfare. The battering rams were contained in wheeled huts that both protected the ram itself and carried archers who could shoot at attackers.

The preferred tactic in conquering a new region was to choose one particular city and lay siege to it. Once a breach in the city's walls was made, the army poured through and proceeded to massacre both the defenders and the citizens. The mutilated bodies would then be hung on the city's walls as a warning to others.

A battering ram is shown breaking down the walls of a city in this bronze relief from the ninth century BCE.

plexes of halls built around two central courtyards and connected by a narrow throne room measuring 65 by 33 feet (9.8 by 10 m). This double architectural design may reflect Aramaean influence.

Art of intimidation

The state rooms and living quarters of the palace at Nimrud were decorated with murals carved out of limestone blocks, each measuring around 6.5 feet (2 m) high and 13 feet (4 m) wide. Many of these murals showed mythological scenes, but there were also scenes of war, which were intended to intimidate those who saw them. In the throne room, there was a continuous pageant of images, in which the king was the main character. The king was shown as the upholder and protector of fertility, a typical motif in Mesopotamia and, indeed, the entire ancient world.

These royal reliefs are unique in terms of their style and content. For the first time, each image portrays a historical event. Many of these wall reliefs were painted in bright colors, representing the absolute height of Mesopotamian art. Above the friezes were more highly colored murals painted directly on to the plaster of the walls. The calibre of the work is all the more remarkable because most of the craftsmen working on the palace were prisoners of war or forced labor conscripted from the far-flung reaches of the empire.

The entrances to the halls and courtyards were guarded by massive three-dimensional sculptures of bull figures with wings and human heads. These figures had the purpose both of protecting the palace against evil spirits and of warning those who came within the palace precincts that the power of the Assyrian king reached far and wide.

In 879 BCE, Ashurnasirpal celebrated the completion of his royal palace by giving an enormous banquet, to which

he invited almost 70,000 guests. The festivities lasted for ten days, during which time 14,000 sheep were consumed and 10,000 vessels of wine were drunk.

A warlike king

Ashurnasirpal's son, Shalmaneser III (ruled c. 858–824 BCE), was as ruthless as Ashurnasirpal and continued his expansionist policies. Shalmaneser crossed the Euphrates 25 times to do battle against the Aramaeans, conducting 32 campaigns in 35 years. However, not all his campaigns were successful. Although Shalmaneser managed to conquer northern Syria, he was unable to subdue

This relief shows an angel or spirit, one of many mythological beings depicted in Assyrian art.

215

Damascus, even though his army besieged the city in 841 BCE. Shalmaneser also campaigned against a new kingdom in the north, Urartu, which was threatening Assyria.

Shalmaneser completed the construction of Nimrud begun by his father and built many other temples and palaces throughout the empire. He commissioned sculptors and artists to produce statues and stelae, including the famous Black Obelisk (see box, page 213), which shows the kings of Israel paying tribute to Assyria. The reliefs in hammered bronze, called the Bronze Gates of Balawat, which once decorated the temple doors in the town of Balawat, northeast of Nimrud, depicted Shalmaneser's victories over the Phoenicians as well as other subjugated territories. The bronze reliefs also showed the rulers of both Tyre and Sidon bringing tribute.

Under Shalmaneser's immediate successors, Assyria entered a period of decline. There was increasing civil unrest, and in the provinces, some of the nobles who held vast territories acted as if they were independent rulers. Over the generations, thousands of Aramaeans who had been transported to Assyria to work on building projects had been assimilated into Assyrian society, and many of them rose to high positions in the civil service. As a result, the Assyrian language was gradually replaced by Aramaic in common usage.

This bronze bowl, made in the eighth century BCE, is believed to be of Phoenician origin, even though it was found at Nimrud. Archaeologists believe that the bowl was brought back to Assyria as war booty.

Coup d'état

In the middle of the eighth century BCE, a military coup brought a new king to the throne. Tiglath-pileser III (ruled c. 746–727 BCE) embarked energetically on restoring and expanding the empire. To this end, he created a regular standing army. Instead of conscripting farmers each year for a campaign, he formed an army of professionals, consisting largely of foreign contingents, with chariots and cavalry as its core. To break the power of the provincial governors, he reduced the size of the provinces. He also abolished tax exemptions for temples and major cities so taxation would be spread more evenly.

After he had restored civil order at home, Tiglath-pileser embarked on a campaign to drive the Urartians out of Syria. Once he had defeated the Urartian army in battle, he besieged the Syrian capital of Arpad, which had become an ally of Urartu. After three years, he took the city. In true Assyrian style, he put all the inhabitants to the sword and razed the city itself to the ground. Then, instead of appointing a local king as his vassal, Tiglath-pileser appointed an Assyrian governor. He then invaded Israel, annexing large territories there, and took Damascus in 732 BCE. By his campaigns, he extended the empire to the Taurus Mountains in the north and the Sinai Desert in the south.

Tiglath-pileser quickly turned his attention to Babylonia. Following the death of the king Nabu-nasir, the Babylonian throne had been claimed by an Aramaean. Tiglath-pileser drove out the Aramaeans and had himself crowned king of Babylon—under the name of Pulu—in 729 BCE. This action united Assyria and Babylonia under one rule.

In the subsequent years, Tiglath-pileser devoted himself to rebuilding and improving Nimrud and its palace. He commissioned new reliefs, many of them showing gruesome scenes of battles and executions, for the palace walls. After his death, he was succeeded by his son Shalmaneser V (ruled c. 727–722 BCE), who spent three years vainly besieging Samaria, the capital of Israel. He proved to be more successful in conquering the rest of the country, but a revolt in Ashur put an end to the reign of Shalmaneser.

Sargon II

The next great ruler of Assyria was Sargon II, who ruled between 722 and 705 BCE. It is not clear exactly who Sargon was, but he may have been a younger brother of Shalmaneser V. In taking the name Sargon, which means "legitimate king," he may have been trying to bolster a weak claim to the throne. To curry favor with the priests and merchants, the first thing he did at the beginning of his reign was to restore some of the privileges they had lost under Tiglath-pileser, particularly the tax exemptions

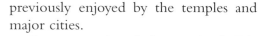

The Black Obelisk of Shalmaneser III, made in the ninth century BCE, is decorated with scenes of the king receiving tribute.

previously enjoyed by the temples and major cities.

Sargon continued the empire building of his predecessor and added further territories. He subjugated Urartu once again and took Carchemish. In 712 BCE, he defeated a coalition of the Syrian and Phoenician cities, annexing numerous states in Syria and southern Anatolia. He campaigned against the Medes on the eastern border and defeated the Aramaeans in the central Tigris Valley and the Chaldeans in the lower Euphrates Valley. In the subjugated regions, Sargon built mighty fortresses.

At the time of Sargon's accession, the throne of Babylonia had been seized by a Chaldean, Merodach-baladan II. Not until 710 BCE did Sargon find the time to move on the usurper, who fled. Merodach-baladan had been so unpopular with the Babylonians that they welcomed Sargon with relief, and he became the first Assyrian to be crowned king of Babylon under his own name.

By this time, Sargon's vast empire extended from the border of Egypt in the southwest to the Zagros Mountains in the east and from the Taurus Mountains in the northwest to the Persian Gulf in the southeast. Sargon divided this empire into some 70 provinces, each headed by a governor who was directly responsible to the king. In his capital of Nimrud, Sargon created a central administrative organization and delegated some of his own power to his son Sennacherib.

Toward the end of his reign, Sargon started on the

construction of a new capital, the famous city of Khorsabad, 8 miles (12.9 km) north of Nineveh. This city was originally called Dur Sharrukin (meaning "Sargon's Fortress"), and it was intended to be more elegant and refined than earlier Assyrian building complexes. However, following Sargon's death in 705 BCE, work on the new capital ceased, and when archaeologists first discovered the site in 1840 CE, the city was just as it had been when it was abandoned 2,500 years earlier.

Under Sargon II, Assyria had reached the peak of its power. However, in 705 BCE, during a minor campaign in western Iran, Sargon was ambushed and slain. His body was left unburied to be eaten by vultures. This inglorious death made a great impression on the world, and his son Sennacherib (ruled 704–681 BCE)

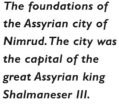

The foundations of the Assyrian city of Nimrud. The city was the capital of the great Assyrian king Shalmaneser III.

ordered his priests to find out what his father had done to incur the wrath of the gods. The priests' answer was that the gods had been offended by the construction of the new capital.

Trouble in Babylon

Before Sargon's death, Sennacherib had quarreled with his father, and on ascending the throne, he seemed determined to turn his back on his late father's memory. He abandoned the half-built city of Dur Sharrukin and, after residing in Ashur for a few years, made Nineveh his capital. In all the many inscriptions of Sennacherib's reign, there is no mention of Sargon.

Soon after Sennacherib's accession, there was trouble with Babylon. In 703 BCE, Merodach-baladan attempted to seize the throne again, allying himself

with the city of Elam, Assyria's age-old enemy. After a nine-month campaign, Sennacherib finally succeeded in defeating this coalition, although Merodach-baladan escaped. In order to reassert control, Sennacherib deported more than 200,000 people from southern Mesopotamia and put an Assyrian puppet king on the Babylonian throne.

Turning his attention to the west, Sennacherib then marched into Syria and Palestine and laid siege to Jerusalem. He was hoping to clear the way for his armies to march on Egypt, but Jerusalem would not yield. Eventually, with his army decimated by sickness, Sennacherib was forced to withdraw.

Meanwhile, in Babylon, Merodach-baladan was stirring up a renewed rebellion. Assyria's puppet king allied himself with Merodach-baladan, but Sennacherib lost no time in crushing the revolt and putting his own son on the Babylonian throne. The Elamites continued to foment Babylonian rebellions, and when the Babylonians handed over Sennacherib's

This Babylonian sculpture depicts a musician. Babylonian culture had a profound effect on that of the Assyrians.

A QUEEN'S CURSE

While most of the great archaeological discoveries relating to the Assyrian Empire occurred in the 19th century CE, one happened a lot more recently—in 1989. Workers removing dirt from one of the palaces at Nimrud stumbled across an air vent to a hidden tomb. Further investigation by the Iraqi archaeologist Muzahim Mahmoud Hussein revealed the skeleton of Queen Yabahya, the wife of Tiglath-pileser III.

The skeleton had been buried with around 80 gold items, including personal jewelry, a golden bowl bearing the queen's name, and a number of rosettes that had been sprinkled over her body. However, the tomb also contained a less pleasant surprise—a curse. An inscription on a marble slab warned that anyone who disturbed the queen's resting place would suffer an eternity of sleeplessness.

son to the Elamites, Sennacherib acted decisively. In 689 BCE, he inflicted a crushing defeat on both states. He then destroyed the city of Babylon. After plundering and leveling the temples, he had the Euphrates River diverted to flood the ruins. In a symbolic act, statues of the gods of the holy city were taken to Ashur as prisoners. This sacrilege offended even some Assyrians, who feared retribution from the Babylonian god Marduk for the deliberate violation of his temple.

Rebuilding Nineveh and Babylon

Sennacherib chose Nineveh to be his capital city. He carried out extensive renovations there and built himself a magnificent palace with beautiful gardens. To bring water to these gardens, an immense aqueduct was constructed, using around two million limestone blocks. The palace itself was decorated with many reliefs, some of which showed enormous statues of bulls being transported over land and water. Other scenes showed military life, battles, and the mass deportations of conquered peoples. To make the palace of Sennacherib as splendid as possible, Assyrian artists were given a free rein in its design.

In 681 BCE, Sennacherib was suddenly assassinated—widely seen as just retribution for his treatment of the god Marduk. Sennacherib was succeeded by his son Esarhaddon (ruled 680–669 BCE).

Esarhaddon was not the eldest son, and it is thought that he owed his throne to the influence of his mother, Naqia. She was a princess from western Syria and, for a long time, controlled state affairs from behind the scenes. To appease Marduk, Esarhaddon set about recon-

structing Babylon, in particular the temples of Marduk. In the west, Esarhaddon attacked Egypt, capturing Memphis in 671 BCE. This victory was the major military achievement of his reign; he died during a second expedition to Egypt in 669 BCE.

The last great king

Once again, Naqia arranged the succession, placing her youngest grandson, Ashurbanipal (ruled c. 668–627 BCE), on the throne and appointing one of his older brothers viceroy of Babylon. Ashurbanipal continued his father's Egyptian campaign, putting down revolts and conquering as far south as Thebes. However, later in Ashurbanipal's reign, the Egyptians succeeded in regaining their independence and driving out the Assyrian garrisons.

In southern Babylonia, the Elamites continued their attacks. Ashurbanipal dispatched an army to defeat them, but his brother, the Babylonian viceroy, rebelled and a protracted war ensued.

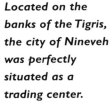

Located on the banks of the Tigris, the city of Nineveh was perfectly situated as a trading center.

The Assyrians laid siege to Babylon for three years. The city was taken in 648 BCE, and the palace was burned to the ground with the viceroy inside.

Determined to subdue the Elamites once and for all, Ashurbanipal invaded their territory and attacked the capital, Susa. The city fell in 646 BCE, after which the Assyrians totally destroyed it and annexed the whole state. This victory was to be the Assyrians' last great military success; thereafter, the empire went into rapid decline.

Ashurbanipal was a man of many talents. Besides being an able military commander and an enthusiastic hunter of big game, he was a mathematician and scientist and was able to read both Sumerian and Akkadian. At his palace at Nineveh, he founded a library in which several copies of the more important works were kept. The library consisted of approximately 25,000 clay tablets, which included new copies of a large number of old texts. This remarkable archive has been a valuable source of Assyrian history for archaeologists.

End of an empire

In the last years of Ashurbanipal's life, civil war broke out between his twin sons. The weakened empire was not able to withstand an onslaught from the Medes, who captured the city of Ashur in 614 BCE. With the help of the Babylonians, the Medes took Nineveh in 612 BCE and razed it to the ground. The Assyrian army, under the last Assyrian king, Ashur-uballit II (ruled 612–609 BCE), fled to Harran in the west. When the Assyrian army was finally defeated at Harran in 609 BCE, the defeat marked the end of the Assyrian Empire.

See also:

The Babylonians (volume 1, page 110)

THE ISRAELITES

The Israelites were a Semitic people who lived in the eastern Mediterranean region. The stories contained in the Old Testament of the Bible are an important source of information about the Israelites' history.

The Israelites of the Bible were descended from pastoral nomads, originally from Arabia, who from around 3000 BCE onwards settled in Mesopotamia, along the eastern coast of the Mediterranean Sea, and in the delta of the Nile River. These nomads were Semites, speakers of Semitic languages, such as Hebrew and Arabic.

In southern Mesopotamia, Semitic nomads settled alongside the Sumerians and later established the Akkadian dynasty—founded by Sargon of Akkad around 2300 BCE. The Akkadians conquered a string of prominent city-states including Ur and Umma. In Syria, Semitic groups established powerful kingdoms at Ebla and Mari.

The land of Canaan

Another Semitic group settled along the eastern shores of the Mediterranean. The long strip of largely fertile land that stretched from southern Anatolia southward to the border with Egypt is known in the Bible as Canaan. Much of Old Testament history records strife between the Canaanites (the earliest Semitic inhabitants of Canaan) and later arrivals, who included the Israelites' ancestors, the Hebrews.

By the 12th century BCE, the Canaanites' kingdom was reduced to the narrow piece of coastal territory that makes up modern Lebanon. Around that time, the eastern Mediterranean coast and Egypt came under repeated attacks from armed raiders who were known to the Egyptians as the Sea Peoples— because they came by boat. Among the raiders were the Philistines, who may have come from Crete. The Philistines proved to be persistent enemies of the Israelites. In biblical accounts, the Philistines are presented as boorish and uncultured, although there is no historical evidence that they lacked artistic ability or interest. The Philistines gave their name to the much-contested land of Palestine.

From the 12th century BCE to the ninth century BCE, the Phoenicians, descendants of earlier Semitic occupants of Canaan, rose to prominence in this coastal area of Canaan. They established a wide commercial empire, with trading posts as far afield as Spain and northern Africa. They were brilliant navigators and expert boatbuilders. In 814 BCE, they founded the great ancient city of Carthage in northern Africa. The city became one of the most important trading powers of the Mediterranean region.

This mosaic from the Basilica of San Marco in Venice depicts the head of Solomon, king of the Israelites. He is most famous for building the temple in Jerusalem. The mosaic was created in the 14th century CE.

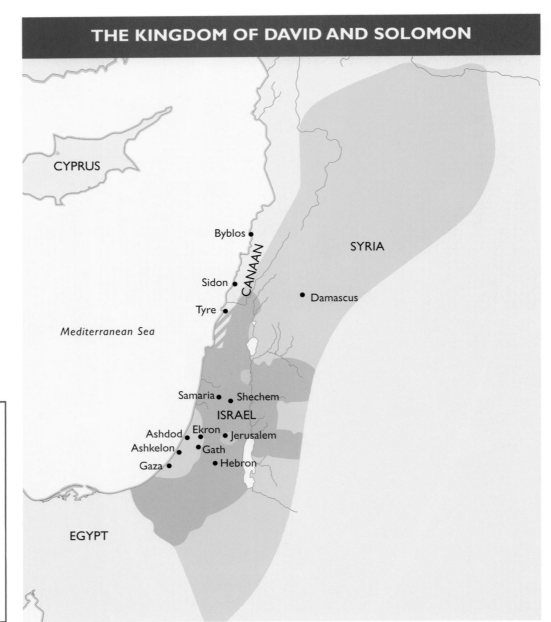

THE KINGDOM OF DAVID AND SOLOMON

CYPRUS

Byblos

CANAAN

SYRIA

Sidon

Damascus

Tyre

Mediterranean Sea

Samaria Shechem

ISRAEL

Ashdod Ekron Jerusalem

Ashkelon Gath

Gaza Hebron

EGYPT

KEY

Area under direct rule (c. 1000–928 BCE)

Vassal states (c. 1000–928 BCE)

Canaanite enclaves conquered by David

Area ceded to Tyre by Solomon

The origins of the Israelites

Out of the many Semitic nomads, one group—the Hebrews—later came to be known as the Israelites. According to the Bible, both Semites and Hebrews were named after ancestors—the Semites because they could all trace their ancestry back to Shem, eldest son of Noah, who built the Ark and survived the Great Flood; the Hebrews because they were all descended from Heber, one of Shem's great-grandsons.

The earliest historical reference to the Hebrews (under the name Hapiru) is found in the so-called Mari tablets. Made around 1800 BCE, these clay records were found in the remains of the palace of King Zimrilim at Mari, a Mesopotamian city on the Euphrates River (now Tall al-Hariri in Syria). The earliest historical reference to Israel and the Israelites comes much later, around 1209 BCE, in the Merneptah stele—a carved stone column recording the achievements of an ancient Egyptian pharaoh, Merneptah, who ruled between 1213 and 1203 BCE. The stele gives an account of Merneptah's victory in battle over Libyan troops and the armies of the Sea Peoples, and it mentions his defeat in western Canaan of forces from Ashkelon, Gezer, Yanoam, and Israel. It declares: "Canaan is taken prisoner and in despair. Ashkelon is defeated, Gezer taken, Yanoam reduced to nothing; Israel also is brought to ruin, its people slain."

Almost all knowledge of the Israelites' earliest history and first migrations comes from the Book of Genesis—the first book of the Hebrew Bible and of the Old Testament in the Christian Bible. This biblical account identifies one man, Abraham (originally called Abram), as the ancestor from whom all the Israelites were descended and as the founder of their religion, Judaism.

Abram's journey to Canaan

According to the Bible, Abram lived in the city of Ur on the lower reaches of the Euphrates River in southern Mesopotamia, probably around 1800 BCE. Located on the same site as modern Tall al-Muqayyar, around 200 miles (300 km) southeast of Baghdad in Iraq, Ur was one of Sumer's major city-states, an important cultural and commercial center.

Abram, according to the account in Genesis, initially left Ur in the company of his wife Sarai (later called Sarah), his nephew Lot, and his father Terah and traveled as far as Harran, which was an ancient pilgrimage site for devotees of the Sumerian moon god Nanna and is now located in southeast Turkey. After staying at Haran for some time, and following the death of Terah, Abram was visited by God (the single god, Yahweh, later worshipped by the Israelites) and instructed to journey to a new land and found a great nation. Abram obeyed and

departed to Canaan. His party made its first encampment in Canaan at Shechem. Genesis adds: "And the Canaanites were then in the land."

God promised the land of Canaan to Abram's descendants, but Abram was childless; his wife Sarai was unable to bear children. Initially, Abram adopted a manservant, Eliezer, as his heir. Then, Sarai gave Abram her maidservant, a young Egyptian woman named Hagar. Abram and Hagar had a son, Ishmael. Subsequently, God declared his intention

The victory stele of Merneptah (an Egyptian pharaoh) contains the earliest recorded mention of the Israelites. It was made around 1209 BCE.

225

The Sacrifice of Isaac, painted in 1604 CE by Caravaggio, depicts the moment when an angel sent by God prevents Abraham from sacrificing his son Isaac.

to make Abram the "father of many nations" and again agreed an "everlasting covenant" with him to give Abram and his descendants the land of Canaan. God declared that Abram should be known as Abraham and Sarai as Sarah and promised that Sarah would bear Abraham a son. It would be with this child that God would keep his covenant.

Sarah's son, Isaac, was the father of Jacob, who is celebrated in Judaism as the forefather of the Jews. Hagar's son, Ishmael, on the other hand, is celebrated in Islam as the forefather of the Arab peoples. Both Abraham (Ibrahim) and Ishmael are viewed as prophets.

Israel's ties with Egypt

The biblical account of the history of the Israelites continues with a description of how Isaac's son Jacob tricked his twin brother Esau out of his birthright and fled to his uncle, Laban, back at Harran. Jacob married Laban's daughters, Leah and Rachel. They and their servants bore Jacob the 12 sons who traditionally established the twelve tribes of Israel. Jacob and his extended family subsequently left Harran and returned to Canaan. On the way, after a nocturnal encounter with an angel of God, Jacob received the new name of Israel. After some time in Canaan, Israel, probably

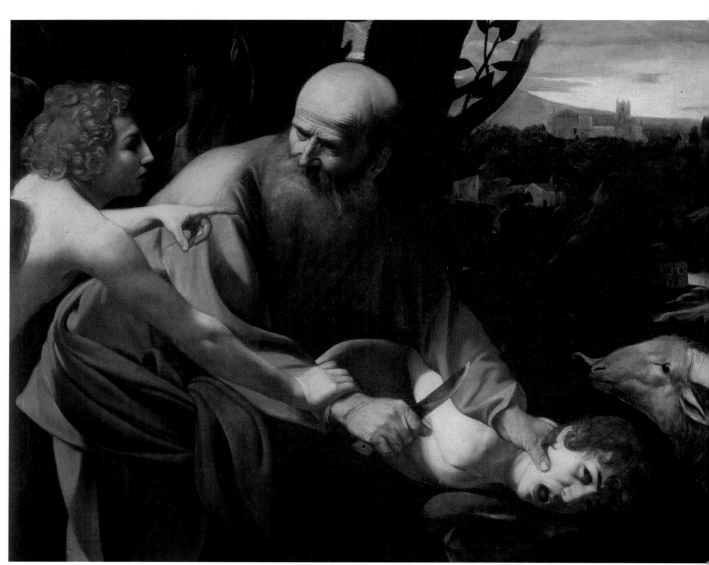

THE TRIBES OF ISRAEL

According to biblical accounts, Jacob (later known as Israel) had 13 children (12 boys and a girl) by his two wives, Leah and Rachel, and their two maidservants, Bilhah (Rachel's servant) and Zilpah (Leah's servant). Leah bore six sons, Reuben, Simeon, Levi, Judah, Issachar, and Zebulun, and a daughter, Dinah. Rachel's sons were Joseph and Benjamin. Bilhah's sons were Dan and Naphtali, while Zilpah's sons were Gad and Asher.

The descendants of the 12 sons of Jacob later formed the 12 Tribes of Israel. Following the Exodus from Egypt and the entry into the Promised Land, Joshua divided the land of Canaan among the tribes. However, the tribe of Levi did not receive any land because the members were hereditary priests. In listings that record land apportioned to the tribes, the tribe of Levi does not appear and the tribe of Joseph is replaced by two tribes, those of his sons Ephraim and Manasseh.

Subsequently, when Israel divided following the death of Solomon, the northern Kingdom of Israel, based on Shechem, was founded by the tribes of Reuben, Simeon, Levi, Issachar, Zebulun, Dan, Naphtali, Gad, Asher, and Ephraim and Manasseh, while the southern Kingdom of Judah was founded by the tribes of Judah and Benjamin. When the northern kingdom was conquered by Assyria in 722 BCE, those tribes were driven into exile in Khorasan (a region of northern Persia) and thereafter lost to history. In religious and cultural tradition, they are remembered as the "ten lost tribes of Israel." A large number of ethnic and religious groups have claimed to be their descendants. The tribes of Judah and Benjamin (and a few of the landless priests, the Levi), who in 586 BCE were driven from Jerusalem into captivity in Babylon, later returned to reestablish their kingdom and rebuild their temple in Jerusalem. They are believed to be the ancestors of all modern Jews.

fleeing famine, left with his extended family for the fertile soil of the Nile Delta in Egypt, where his descendants, "the children of Israel," remained for many centuries.

Many historians believe that the stories of Jacob's travels are rooted in the early history of the Israelites. These historians agree that some of the Hebrew tribes migrated to Egypt, probably during the mid-17th to the mid-16th centuries BCE. During this period, the Semitic Hyksos kings (probably from Canaan) conquered the northernmost part of Egypt. However, when the Hyksos rulers were deposed in the 16th century BCE, the Hebrews were persecuted and treated as slaves.

Exodus

The children of Israel were led out of captivity in Egypt by a great religious and political leader named Moses. The Old Testament account of their escape details the Ten Plagues that afflicted Egypt, the Passover of the Angel of God that spared first-born Hebrew children, 40 years of wandering the desert, and the handing down at Mount Sinai of God's Ten Commandments (see box, page 228). These events are presented as key elements in the formation of the Israelites' national and religious identity. The date of the Exodus or escape from Egypt is not certain, but many scholars believe that it took place in the 13th century BCE, during the reign of

MOSES AND THE HEBREWS' EXODUS FROM EGYPT

According to the Old Testament books of Exodus and Deuteronomy, Moses—the man who led the Hebrews out of captivity in Egypt—was born to Hebrew parents in Goshen, Egypt. His mother put Moses in a basket made of papyrus and floated it on the river to save him from the pharaoh's order to put all male Hebrew infants to death. The pharaoh's daughter found and raised Moses, and he rose to a position of prominence in the Egyptian government. However, when he saw an Egyptian overseer beat a Hebrew, Moses killed the boorish overseer in a fit of rage and fled into the Sinai Desert to escape retribution. Moses lived there for some time with Semitic nomads and had his first visions of Yahweh, the God of Abraham, Isaac, and Jacob. Yahweh appeared to Moses in a burning bush and commanded him to return to Egypt and lead his people to freedom.

Moses leads the Israelites out of Egypt, while the pursuing Egyptian army is drowned in the Red Sea. The biblical story of the Israelites' journey is probably based on fact.

The pharaoh refused to allow the captive Israelites to leave, so God sent a series of plagues to Egypt. As the last of these plagues, God killed the first-born children in Egypt, saving only those belonging to the Israelites who had marked their doors with lambs' blood. This event is the origin of the Jewish festival of Passover.

Moses, pursued by the pharaoh's army, led the Israelites out from Egypt, God parted the Red Sea to let the Israelites pass and then allowed the waters to break over and drown the Egyptian pursuers. Afterward, the Israelites wandered in the desert for 40 years. This section of the narrative may represent the Israelites' rediscovery of their nomadic and Semitic roots and their gradual abandonment of Egyptian practices.

When the Israelites reached Mount Sinai, Moses communed with God on the mountaintop for a long period, during which God handed down the Ten Commandments. Above all else, the commandments firmly established the concept of monotheism, for they began with the command: "I am the Lord thy God, who has brought you out of the land of Egypt.... You shall have no other gods but me."

Ramses II (1279–1213 BCE) or the reign of his son and successor Merneptah (1213–1204 BCE). By this date, the children of Israel had been in Egypt for around 300 to 400 years.

Moses led his people out of Egypt and through the desert wilderness of northern Egypt and into Jordan. He saw Canaan from the top of Mount Pisgah but died without reaching the Promised Land. Before his death, Moses turned leadership of the people over to a warrior named Joshua. The Israelites remained in what is now Jordan for some years, on the eastern bank of the river of the same name, but in time, they began to cross over into Canaan, the place described to them in Egypt as "a land flowing with milk and honey."

Religious strife

In Canaan, the Israelites encountered Semitic tribes and isolated groups of Hittites, a people who had founded an empire in the region in the 17th century BCE but whose power was now dwindling. According to the biblical account, God had ordered the eradication of the people of Canaan. Some settlers burned towns and villages and slaughtered the inhabitants, but more often than not, this occupation was peaceful—and the native populace was left alone to coexist peacefully with the Israelites.

The Israelites and Canaanites spoke related Semitic languages and were able

This limestone stele carries a depiction of the god Baal. It was found in the city of Ugarit in Canaan.

easily enough to communicate with each other. Religion became a point of conflict, however. It is clear from biblical accounts that the Israelite settlers did not always keep to their tribal faith—the worship of Yahweh, God of Abraham—and were attracted to local pagan cults. The main deities worshipped in Canaan at this time were the rain and fertility god Baal and Ishtar, a goddess of war and sexual love.

Shiloh

The Israelites set up a sanctuary to Yahweh at Shiloh that contained the Ark of the Covenant. Also referred to as the Ark of the Law, the Ark of the Testimony, or the Ark of God, this wooden chest was, according to biblical accounts, 2.5 cubits (3 feet, 9 inches; 1.15 m) long and 1.5 cubits (2 feet, 3 inches; 0.7 m) wide and high. The Israelites took it with them on military campaigns and carried it into battle on poles. The Ark was said to contain both a pot of manna (the food that God sent to feed the Israelites in the desert after their escape from Egypt) and the stone tablets on which the Ten Commandments were carved.

To many Israelites, Yahweh took on the aspects of a god of war. In addition to the sanctuary at Shiloh, the Israelites worshipped Yahweh at Bethel, Gilgal, Mizpah, and Hebron. The Canaanites built sanctuaries to Baal and Ishtar beside the Israelite sanctuaries.

The first king of Israel

For more than a century, the Israelites lived in Canaan without a common leader, but then the Canaanites and Hittites joined forces to combat a new enemy (the Philistines), and the Israelites had to organize themselves as a unified power. The Philistines, one of the Sea Peoples described in Egyptian documents of the period, ransacked towns along the eastern Mediterranean coast. At first, the Philistines occupied only five coastal towns (Gaza, Ashkelon, Ashdod, Ekron, and Gath), but before long, they began to drive the Israelites and the Canaanites farther and farther inland.

The Israelites gradually made the difficult transition from tribal organization under chiefs or judges to the establishment of a single monarchy. The first king of Israel was Saul, who reigned from around 1021 to 1000 BCE. According to biblical accounts, Saul was chosen as king by the seer Samuel and then acclaimed by the people after winning a great victory over the Ammonites. Control of the tribal chiefs had always been limited, and the transition to a strong monarchy was achieved with great difficulty. Saul had to contend with opposition from within his fledgling kingdom as well as from Israel's enemies, but he largely succeeded in his most important task, that of defending Israel. Saul drove the Philistines back toward the coast and defeated the Amalekites, although his reign ended with a defeat at the hands of the resurgent Philistines on the plains of Gilboa.

David and Solomon

Saul's successor, David, expanded the Kingdom of Israel as far as the Red Sea and the Euphrates River. David also established Jerusalem as the capital of the Israelites. This ancient settlement in the arid mountains of Judaea, 35 miles (56 km) east of the Mediterranean and 15 miles (24 km) to the west of the Dead Sea, was founded around 3000 BCE. It was a possession of the Egyptians around 1800 BCE, and in the Amarna Letters, a collection of Egyptian diplomatic correspondence from around 1400 BCE, it was called Uru-Salem (meaning

This 17th-century-CE engraving by Merian Matthäus the Elder depicts the return of the Ark of the Covenant. The Ark was said to contain the stone tablets on which the Ten Commandments were written.

This relief shows the Assyrian king Sennacherib laying siege to the city of Jerusalem.

"City of Peace"). When David captured the city around 1000 BCE, it was—according to biblical accounts—a stronghold of a Canaanite people called the Jebusites.

David made Jerusalem the center of the Israelite religion. The city consisted of two hills separated by a ravine. Most of the people lived on the western hill, while David established his own royal quarters on the eastern hill, which became known as Zion. David intended to build a great temple and palace, but he died before he could bring the plans to fruition. However, his son King Solomon, using the best Phoenician architects and craftsmen and the finest materials from Lebanon, constructed a superb temple and palace complex in the mid-10th century BCE.

Solomon allied himself with the Phoenician king Hiram of Tyre, who sent a merchant fleet to Ophir (possibly modern Arabia) every three years. Hiram sent sailors and shipbuilders, while Solomon provided the harbor of Ezion-Geber (Elat) on the eastern arm of the Red Sea, conquered in King David's reign, and traded with Seba (probably southern Arabia). The arrangement enabled Solomon to procure the means to maintain a magnificent court during the highest point of power and importance for ancient Israel and its monarchy.

Israel and Judah under attack

After Solomon's death around 928 BCE, Israel divided into two hostile kingdoms. The main group of the 12 tribes of Israel, fed up with the extravagance of Solomon, rejected the rule of Solomon's son Rehoboam and established the northern Kingdom of Israel, with its capital at Shechem (soon superseded by Samaria) and religious sanctuaries at Dan and Bethel. The tribes of Judah and Benjamin, meanwhile, remained loyal and established the southern Kingdom of Judah, with Jerusalem as its capital and holy city.

Before long, however, Israel and Judah came under attack from the rising powers of Assyria and Babylonia. In 722 BCE, an Assyrian army led by King Sargon II captured Samaria, by then the capital of Israel, and drove thousands of the children of Israel into exile. In 701 BCE, Sennacherib, Sargon's son and successor, led Assyrian armies against the southern Kingdom of Judah. After many brutal victories, Sennacherib besieged Jerusalem but failed to capture it.

The respite for the people of Judah was relatively brief. A little more than a century later, in 586 BCE, Nebuchadnezzar, the king of Babylon, captured Jerusalem, destroying the city and razing the Temple of Solomon to the ground.

See also:

The Assyrians (volume 2, page 208) • Egypt's New Kingdom (volume 1, page 92) • The Phoenicians (volume 2, page 196)

THE PERSIANS

The Persian Empire flourished from the late seventh century BCE until the late fourth century BCE. The empire reached the height of its power during the reigns of Cyrus the Great and his successors Cambyses II, Darius I, and Xerxes.

The Persians were originally a nomadic Indo-European people who settled on the Iranian plateau. From the middle of the sixth century BCE, they embarked on a campaign of conquest that enabled them to build an enormous empire, extending from Egypt and Anatolia in the west to northwestern India in the east. It was the largest empire the world had ever known and was to last until 330 BCE, when it fell to the Macedonian king Alexander the Great.

The heartland of this great empire was a vast plateau in southwestern Asia surrounded by volcanic mountain ranges interspersed with some lowlands. Sometime during the third millennium BCE, a hardy people, along with their horses and sheep, spread from the grasslands of central Asia to settle on this plateau between the Persian Gulf and the Caspian Sea. They called themselves Aryans, or Irani, and they called their new homeland Irania (present-day Iran). These people later came to be called Persians because of a mistake made by the Greeks, who named them after the province of Parsa.

The Medes

These Indo-European people gradually abandoned their nomadic lifestyle and settled down as farmers and cattle herders. One group—the Persians— stayed on the plateau; another group— the Indians—moved on to a region on the Indian subcontinent between the Indus and Ganges rivers. Around 700 BCE, a number of tribes on the plateau attempted to form a kingdom. These people were the Medes. According to the Greek historian Herodotus, the first Median king was Deioces. Although the accuracy of this account is not certain, it seems that Deioces established a capital for the new kingdom at Ekbatana (present-day Hamadan).

A later Median king, Phraortes, ruled from around 675 to 653 BCE. Leading an army of Median tribes, all carrying only a long spear and a wicker shield, Phraortes braved the might of the Assyrians, meeting them in a battle in 653 BCE. However, the Medes were defeated and Phraortes was slain. He was succeeded by his son Cyaxares, who modernized the army and added bows and arrows to its arsenal of weapons. Cyaxares succeeded in banishing a northern nomadic people known as the Scythians, who had invaded Median territory in his father's reign, and in 612 BCE, with the help of the Babylonians, Cyaxares captured Nineveh, the Assyrian capital. The city was thoroughly destroyed and never rebuilt. The loss of Nineveh marked the beginning of the downfall of the Assyrian Empire.

The last Median king was Astyages, son of Cyaxares. Astyages inherited a large kingdom from his father, including the vassal kingdoms of the Persians. Despite his long reign from 585 to 550 BCE, Astyages, preferring a life of luxury, did little to consolidate his empire. He did, however, marry his daughter to the Persian king, Cambyses I. In 559 BCE, that couple's son became the Persian vassal king Cyrus II.

Cyrus the Great

Cyrus II was descended from the Persian king Achaemenes, and for this reason, the Persian dynasty he was to found was called the Achaemenids. Cyrus was ambitious to restore the fortunes of the Persians, and soon after he became king, he united several Persian and Iranian tribes and led a revolt against Astyages. An army with Astyages at its head set out to quell the rebellion, but when the army

This relief from around the sixth century BCE depicts two sphinxes, animals that are commonly seen in art from the Persian Empire.

233

reached the capital of Parsa, the generals mutinied and handed Astyages over to Cyrus. In 550 BCE, the triumphant Persians captured Ekbatana and seized its treasury of gold and silver.

The Persians under Cyrus had routed the Medes, and the vanquished Median Empire now became the Persian Empire. However, the Persians did not wreak vengeance upon the Median people. Under Persian rule, Medes were often appointed to high official positions and even given commands in the Persian army.

Conquest of Lydia

In the far west of Anatolia, King Croesus of Lydia heard of the fall of the Median Empire and took the opportunity to invade former Median territory with the hope of extending his own kingdom. Legend has it that Croesus consulted the oracle at Delphi in Greece before setting out on his campaign. In answer to his question about whether it was wise to go to war, Croesus was told that if he crossed the Halys River (the border with the former Median Empire) to engage with the Persians, an empire would fall. Unfortunately, he did not realize that the doomed empire was his own.

Eager to defend the borders of his new empire (and probably eager also to capture Croesus's immense treasury of gold), Cyrus drove Croesus back across the Halys River and pushed on into Lydia. On a small plain near the Lydian capital of Sardis, Cyrus's army was confronted by a troop of Lydian cavalry armed with spears. Taking the advice of his general, Cyrus brought to the front the camels that were carrying the army's baggage. The enemy horses took fright at the camels' horrible smell, turned tail, and bolted. Cyrus forced the remnants of the Lydian army back into Sardis and then laid siege to the city. After two weeks, his engineers succeeded in scaling the walls. The city was taken, and Croesus was captured. Cyrus put Croesus to death and annexed Lydia and the Greek coastal cities of Ionia that had previously been subject to Lydia.

Turning east, Cyrus set his sights on Babylon. A successful campaign through the Iranian lands had not only doubled the size of his empire but also swelled the ranks of his army with soldiers drawn from the defeated regions. His march on Babylon was largely unopposed, since the country was suffering from the weak rule of the scholarly King Nabonidus. Famine threatened the peasants, and the population was looking for someone to deliver it from its predicament. Cyrus reached Babylon in October of 539 BCE and took the city without a battle.

Cyrus was in possession of the whole Babylonian Empire, which included Syria and Palestine. He proved himself to be a benevolent ruler and was soon popular with the Babylonians. He rebuilt the ruined temples and restored statues of the gods (which had been removed by Nabonidus) to their rightful places. Cyrus also decreed that the Jews, who had been exiled to Babylon from Palestine, were free to return home and that the temple in Jerusalem (which had been destroyed by the Babylonian kings) should be rebuilt and its gold and silver utensils should be restored.

Cyrus established his capital city at Pasargadae, in the southern part of Iran. His palace there was set in a park and contained a great hall fronted by an impressive porch consisting of two rows of 20 wooden columns, each 20 feet (6 m) high. The park later contained his tomb, which was constructed from huge blocks of white limestone and bore the inscription "Here I lie, Cyrus, king of kings." The last years of Cyrus's reign were spent defending his eastern frontier, where he was killed in battle in 529 BCE.

THE GROWTH OF THE PERSIAN EMPIRE

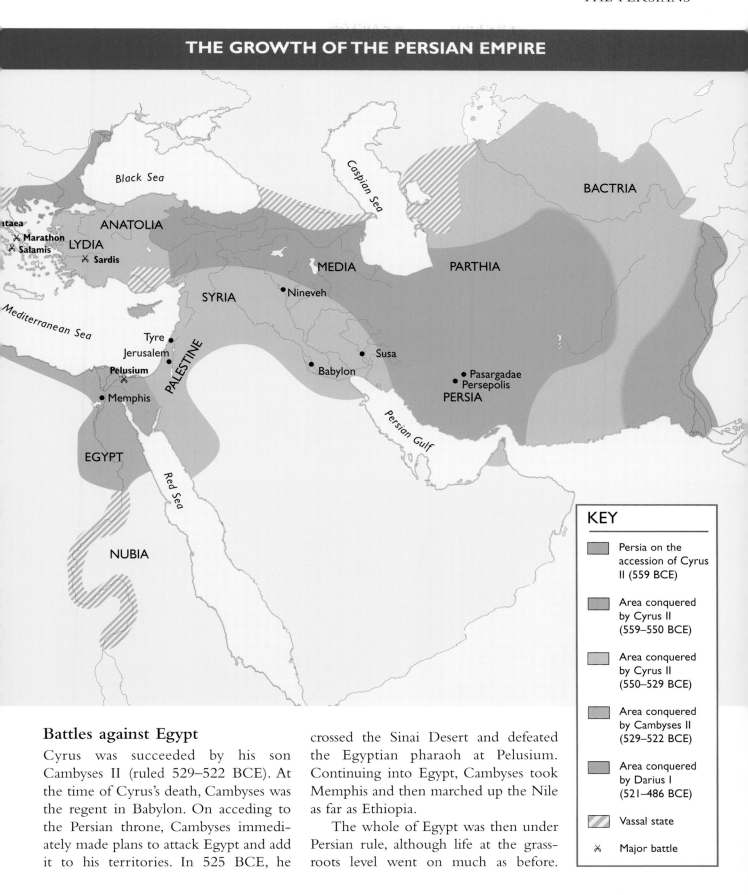

KEY

Persia on the accession of Cyrus II (559 BCE)

Area conquered by Cyrus II (559–550 BCE)

Area conquered by Cyrus II (550–529 BCE)

Area conquered by Cambyses II (529–522 BCE)

Area conquered by Darius I (521–486 BCE)

Vassal state

✕ Major battle

Battles against Egypt

Cyrus was succeeded by his son Cambyses II (ruled 529–522 BCE). At the time of Cyrus's death, Cambyses was the regent in Babylon. On acceding to the Persian throne, Cambyses immediately made plans to attack Egypt and add it to his territories. In 525 BCE, he crossed the Sinai Desert and defeated the Egyptian pharaoh at Pelusium. Continuing into Egypt, Cambyses took Memphis and then marched up the Nile as far as Ethiopia.

The whole of Egypt was then under Persian rule, although life at the grassroots level went on much as before.

Cambyses honored the Egyptian gods and restored their temples, although he did substantially reduce the revenues allotted to the temples. This reduction of the temple revenues may have earned Cambyses his reputation as a harsh ruler.

In 522 BCE, Cambyses learned that his brother Bardiya had seized control of the empire. Cambyses hastily set out back to Persia to quell this revolt, but he died on the way. It was left to a young prince of the Achaemenid line, Darius, to put down the rebellion and claim the empire for himself.

The reign of Darius I

At the beginning of 522 BCE, Darius (ruled 521–486 BCE) was 28 years of age and, according to the Greek historian Herodotus, one of the king's spear-bearers in Egypt. It seems likely that as soon as Cambyses died, Darius left the army and hastened back to Media to join with a party of nobles to usurp the usurper.

After almost two years of civil strife all over the empire, Darius finally succeeded in quelling all opposition and took the Persian throne as Darius I. On the Behistun Inscription (see box, page 243) Darius claimed his right to rule through his descent from princes of the royal blood. Darius also claimed that Cambyses had slain Bardiya before going to Egypt and that it was an imposter, Gaumatan, who had rebelled in Bardiya's name.

The first imperative for Darius on ascending the throne was to restore order in a war-torn empire. Darius was an able administrator, and he set about restoring and strengthening the system of satrapies (provinces) that had been instituted by Cyrus II. The empire was divided into 20 satrapies, each a vast territory ruled over by a satrap (governor) who was directly responsible to the king. Each province also had a military commander who took instructions directly from the king, thereby ensuring military supervision of the whole empire. In addition,

The palace of Cyrus the Great at Pasargadae. Pasargadae was the first capital of the Persian Empire.

THE PERSIAN ARMY

The Persian army of the sixth and fifth centuries BCE was, at that time, the most massive army that had ever existed. At one point in time, the army is said to have comprised more than a million soldiers, although such claims are probably exaggerated. All subjugated people had to supply troops to Persia, which resulted in an army that consisted of groups of foreign soldiers who each had trained to fight with different weapons and with different strategies.

The king had three units of royal troops, each consisting of 2,000 horsemen and 2,000 infantry, and an elite regiment of 10,000 soldiers called the Immortals. These Immortals were the king's personal bodyguard, and their number never fell below 10,000; there was always a replacement ready to step into the shoes of any Immortal who became ill or died. The uniform of the Immortals was richly decorated with gold, and each soldier carried a spear, a bow, and a quiver of arrows. The members of this privileged regiment were allowed to take servants and concubines along on campaigns.

The provinces all had to supply their own contingents of troops, which were divided into squads, companies, regiments, and brigades that consisted of ten, one hundred, one thousand, and ten thousand troops respectively. Altogether, the army of Xerxes had six corps, each under its own corps commander. Many of the provinces also supplied cavalry and charioteers, while the maritime provinces supplied ships and oarsmen for the redoubtable Persian navy. The Persian army on the move was a truly formidable sight, calculated to inspire terror in the hearts of all who saw it.

Darius established a secret service, called "the king's eyes and ears," which consisted of messengers who inspected each province annually and reported back to the king.

Darius also instituted a new legal system to be imposed on the whole empire. In each province, there were to be two courts. One court would hear cases relating to local laws. The other court would deal with cases that came under Persian imperial jurisdiction. The tax system was also revised by Darius. While Persians were only required to pay taxes in times of national emergency, each province had to pay a fixed annual amount of money and goods to the king's treasury. Because of the different harvest sizes in the various provinces, surveyors were sent out to estimate the yield in each province, and taxes were assessed accordingly. Another improvement carried out by Darius was to establish a uniform system of coinage throughout the empire, which, together with standardized weights and measures, greatly simplified the process of collecting taxes.

Territorial expansion

With his empire more or less under control, Darius turned his attention to further expansion. A campaign to the east secured new territories right up to the Indus River. Another campaign in 516 BCE against the Scythians north of the Black Sea was not so successful, and Darius was forced to withdraw. A rebellion by the Greek cities in Ionia in 500 BCE had to be suppressed, and after that, Darius set his sights on the Greek mainland. At first, Darius met with some success. However, he was thoroughly defeated at the Battle of Marathon in 490 BCE. A revolt in Egypt followed, but just as Darius was preparing to move

The tomb of the Persian king Cyrus the Great is located in Pasargadae (in southern Iran), which was the location of Cyrus's palace when he was alive.

rat were demolished, together with many other temples. The golden statue of the god Marduk was removed and melted down, while all the citizens of Babylon saw their possessions confiscated and handed over to the Persians. The policies of Xerxes were in complete contrast to those of earlier Persian kings, who had been tolerant of local gods and religions and who had even rebuilt the local temples on occasion.

In 480 BCE, Xerxes invaded Greece with an army of 70,000 men. At first, the campaign went well, and Athens was captured. However, in a great sea battle at Salamis, the Persians were defeated and lost a third of their fleet. When the Persians were subsequently beaten, this time on land, at the Battle of Plataea in 479 BCE, the campaign petered out, and Xerxes lost interest in any further attempts to expand his empire.

After Xerxes was assassinated in 465 BCE, a century of rebellion and civil war ensued. Various members of the Achaemenid royal house at times gained power and at others plotted against each other. During this period, the empire inevitably suffered; it was never again to know the firm direction it had enjoyed under Darius. Despite its military weakness, Persia did play a significant diplomatic role in the Peloponnesian Wars, which involved Athens and Sparta. Persia supplied first one side and then the other with financial aid in return for political concessions.

The coming of Alexander

When Darius III succeeded to the throne in 336 BCE, he found himself under threat from the might of Alexander the Great of Macedonia, who had already conquered Greece and was eager to extend his empire. Alexander marched on Persia, winning three battles before capturing the capital, Persepolis, in 330 BCE. In triumph, Alexander held

to quell the latest rebellion, he died at the age of 64, leaving his son and successor, Xerxes, to crush the Egyptians.

Xerxes

In contrast to his predecessor, Xerxes (ruled 486–465 BCE) proved himself to be a heavy-handed ruler of Egypt. Ignoring the usual forms of Egyptian rule, he imposed Persian law, riding roughshod over local sensibilities. Xerxes proved equally ruthless when the Babylonians rebelled against Persian rule in 482 BCE. After the city of Babylon was retaken, the fortifications and ziggu-

This relief sculpture of an unidentified man was found at Persepolis and dates to the reign of Darius I.

PERSEPOLIS

Work on the great city of Persepolis was started by Darius I and completed by his son Xerxes. Darius intended the city to be the capital of the Persian Empire, reflecting both its might and wealth. He also wanted a luxurious royal residence fit for an all-powerful king. Darius chose a site a few miles southwest of Pasargadae, the old capital of Cyrus the Great. Work started on the fortifications sometime around 500 BCE. A great perimeter wall was constructed on a natural platform at the base of the Mount of Mercy. The wall consisted of huge limestone blocks topped by mud bricks, bringing the total height in places to 60 feet (18.2 m).

The royal palace was situated on the west side of the citadel. The palace included a large reception hall, called the Apadana, which featured imposing columns of stone up to 65 feet (20 m) high. The columns were topped with ornate capitals

The remains of the palace of Darius at Persepolis. Much of the palace was destroyed by fire on the orders of Alexander the Great.

supporting the timber beams that held up the roof. South of the Apadana were the many private royal apartments, including a harem.

The palace housed many ceremonial gates and stairways, all decorated with elaborate stone carvings, which were carried out by an army of stone carvers, wood carvers, goldsmiths, silversmiths, and other artists. Almost every stone surface carried a carved relief. These magnificent examples of Persian art are nowhere seen to better effect than in the Apadana, where there were scenes of palms and cypresses, lions and bulls, culminating in the depiction of a great procession of nobles, courtiers, soldiers, and representatives of the subject peoples advancing to greet their king.

On the east side of the citadel, Xerxes built a vast throne room that had 10 rows of columns with 10 columns in each row, giving rise to its modern name, the Hall of a Hundred Columns. The hall was entered through a porch on the north side. The porch was held up by 16 columns, each decorated at the top by a bull with a human head. The eight doorways into the hall were all decorated with reliefs.

This palace complex was sacked by Alexander the Great in 330 BCE, and the buildings were put to the torch. According to some sources, Alexander's order to burn the palace was given while he was drunk at a feast and being urged on by his fellow revelers.

The remains of the city of Persepolis, which was the capital of the Persian Empire. The city was famous throughout the ancient world for its riches.

a great feast in the palace at Persepolis—and the next morning burned it to the ground. Persepolis itself—reputedly the richest city under the sun—was looted of its treasures, all the men were put to the sword, and the women were enslaved. In the same year that Persepolis was taken, Darius was murdered, probably by his own followers, and the history of the Persian Empire was at an end.

Religion

The early Persians worshipped a variety of gods, many of whom were associated with natural phenomena, such as the sun. However, around 600 BCE, a great prophet started expounding the tenets of a new religion that recognized just one god, called Ahura Mazda (Lord of Wisdom). The prophet's name was Zoroaster (or Zarathustra), and the religion he preached was eventually to become the official religion of the Persian Empire.

Zoroaster is believed to have lived for around 77 years. The stories told about him testify to his desire to help the poor and unfortunate. In his youth, during a period of great drought, he is said to have distributed his father's stores of food to the poor. On another occasion, he tried to save a half-starved dog and its five pups. When he was 20, he left his parents' house and embarked on a search for the most just and merciful person he could find. He traveled for seven years, and during that time, he began to formulate the ideas behind his new religion.

241

Zoroaster rejected all but one of the many gods of his day. He chose to worship Ahura Mazda as the one all-powerful god, the embodiment of good. Ahura Mazda's adversary was Angra Mainyu, the personification of evil. The world was created, said Zoroaster, in the struggle between the two of them. Since then, the conflict between good and evil, light and dark, has been a never-ending battle.

This bronze harness ring, discovered in the Luristan region of western Iran, was made between the 10th and 7th centuries BCE.

The prophet struggled for many years to persuade people to relinquish their beliefs in the old magic cults and adhere to his new faith. Even though he was not very eloquent, he was determined to free his people from the grip of irrational superstition. "As a priest," he is recorded as saying, "I will continue to search for the paths of righteousness and teach the way to cultivate the earth." It seems he was persecuted for his teachings, and he writes: "To which country shall I flee? Where shall I hide?" For a moment, his faith seems to waver: "Do not desert me Ahura Mazda. Help me as a friend who helps his friends. Teach me to think well and correctly."

Evidently, his prayers were answered. After ten years of preaching, Zoroaster made his first convert—his cousin Maidioman, who became his disciple. Two years later, a local king called Hystaspes also converted and embraced the new religion very enthusiastically. Hystaspes and Zoroaster became close friends, and the king converted his entire court to the new religion. Hystaspes also undertook military campaigns with the aim of imposing the teachings of Zoroaster on neighboring peoples.

Hystaspes was probably only a minor ruler who had to pay tribute to the nomadic Tartars who were his neighbors. Urged on by his new belief and by the prophet, Hystaspes waged two successful holy wars against the Tartars to end this humiliating situation. The triumphs of Hystaspes greatly enhanced the reputation of the faith among the Persian people.

It is believed that Zoroaster was murdered around 550 BCE by fanatic Tartars or by a hostile religious figure defending the old faith. In some legends, the prophet's death is depicted as a supernatural event; he is said to have been carried off to heaven by a flash of lightning to save him from cruel tortures.

The Avesta

Zoroaster's teachings are preserved in the Avesta, the sacred books of Zoroastrianism. The Avesta was compiled around 224 CE and is based on the writings of Zoroaster himself. In it, he preaches a faith in a benevolent god, Ahura Mazda, and describes the eternal conflict between good and evil. The good spirit battles its opposite spirit, which has chosen evil. The first spirit works toward unity and creativity, while the second only seeks to destroy. Human beings, says the prophet, must chose between the two. If they opt for the side of good, they support Ahura Mazda in his work. Ahura Mazda demands right thinking, honesty, devotion, and health (all manifestations of good) from his followers. In his youth, Zoroaster was influenced by the cult of fire, which maintained that all evil on earth would eventually be purified by fire.

According to the writings in the Avesta, the supreme god Ahura Mazda created 16 countries, the first of which was Airyana Vaeja, the cradle of all people. Although described as an area with many good features, this country was endowed with winter and serpents by the evil force, Angra Mainyu. The winter (which was considered to be "the worst of horrors" by Ahura Mazda) lasted for 10 months, while the summer lasted for only 2 months. This duality pervaded the religion. For every good creation of Ahura Mazda, his enemy Angra Mainyu counters with a disaster.

Early migration

After describing the 15 other countries, the Avesta retells a legend linked to the emigration of the early Indo-Europeans from Persia. Yima, the first Indo-European king of a tribal people, takes it upon himself "to extend the country," which is packed with herds, people, and dogs. After leading three attempts to emigrate, Yima goes south toward the sun and touches the earth with his dagger and his seal ring, ordering the earth to expand to twice its size: "Open, earth, and extend yourself in order to feed more people and animals."

According to the Avesta, dogs and cattle were the only domestic animals kept by the Persians as they migrated. Persians held dogs in high esteem and considered them only slightly less developed than humans—the punishment for

THE BEHISTUN INSCRIPTION

One of the most important sources of information about the reign of the Persian king Darius I is an inscription on a rock face in the foothills of the Zagros Mountains. The text is known as the Behistun Inscription, from the ancient name of the nearby town of Bisitun. The location of the inscription is extremely inaccessible.

The inscription lists Darius's ancestors, details his rise to power and his defeat of the imposter Gaumata (who had rebelled in Bardiya's name), and gives accounts of Darius's many victories over peoples such as the Babylonians, the Medes, and the Elamites. The text is accompanied by a life-size carving of Darius standing with his foot on Gaumata's chest.

The Behistun Inscription is important for more than just its content. The text is written three times, once in Old Persian, once in Elamite, and once in Babylonian. The fact that the text was the same in all three cases allowed linguists to translate these languages for the first time.

The first person in modern times to attempt to translate the inscription was Sir Henry Rawlinson, a British soldier and academic who began work on the Old Persian inscription in 1835. He managed a complete translation of the text by 1838. Five years later, Rawlinson returned to Bisitun to copy the other two inscriptions, which were gradually translated during the following years.

Ahura Mazda was the chief god of the Zoroastrian religion. Rituals involving the worship of Ahura Mazda were often performed at outdoor altars. This altar is located in southwestern Iran.

the ill-treatment of dogs and slaves was the same. The Avesta advises owners to feed dogs milk and meat and to punish the dogs as if they were responsible for their behavior. After the first attack by a dog, its right ear was to be cut off; after the second, its left ear; and so on.

Most of the Persian priests belonged to the Median tribe and were called Magi. The Magi adapted many of Zoroaster's teachings and used them for their own purposes. In the Avesta, fragments of Zoroaster's original teachings are found mingled with age-old tales about the evil spirits of the steppes and detailed descriptions of magicians' rites. The Greek historian Herodotus considered many of the Persian rituals to be of Magi origin, including the protection of dogs and the funeral practice of leaving corpses to be destroyed by the elements rather than burying or cremating them.

Lifestyle

Herodotus also provided a description of the Persians' lifestyle, saying that they had no statues of gods, or temples, or altars (although archaeological evidence says otherwise). "They also bring offerings to the god of the sun, the moon, fire, water, and wind," he continues. "Of all the feasts, the most important one for the Persians is their birthday." He goes on to say that after courage, the Persians most admire fertility: "Each year the king sends gifts to the family with the most children." According to Herodotus, children were taught only three things between the ages of 5 and 20—horseback riding, archery, and telling the truth. "The most contemptuous deed is to tell a lie," Herodotus reports, "and after that comes getting into debt. The Persians never pollute the waters of their rivers with garbage, and neither do they wash their hands in them. They consider the rivers to be holy."

Before the rise of their empire, the Persians were still a relatively primitive people. When Croesus of Lydia was preparing to go to war with the Persians around 550 BCE, one of his counselors advised him: "You are going to war against a people who wear leather pants, live off dry ground, drink water rather than wine, and do not know figs. If you conquer them, you will still own nothing. If they vanquish you they will be incredibly rich."

Whatever their reputation, the Persian lifestyle certainly did not exclude a love of wine. The alcoholic tendencies of Cambyses II were legendary, and Herodotus reports of the Persians: "It is their custom to discuss business when they are drunk—but they only make their decisions the next day, when they are sober again."

Despite this dubious press, the Persian kings were on the whole enlightened and benevolent rulers. For the most part, when they conquered a territory, they respected the local customs and gods and often employed local people as officials. Although the regional satrapies had to pay heavy taxes, in return they enjoyed the benefits of the public projects that the Persian government carried out throughout the empire. These projects included improving drainage and irrigation of agricultural land by constructing a system of underground channels to carry water in desert regions. One vast water project carried out during Darius's reign was the building of a great canal to link the Red Sea with the Mediterranean Sea. The journey along the canal took four days to complete.

The Royal Road

The Persians built a great network of roads that made traveling from one part of the empire to another relatively simple. The greatest one of these roads, which was called the Royal Road, covered a distance of 1,550 miles (2,500 km) and linked Sardis in Lydia to the one-time Persian capital of Susa. There were staging posts along all the main routes where travelers could change horses, get a meal, and take some rest. This road network enabled messengers for the king to travel at great speed, keeping him informed of events in even the most remote parts of his empire. The network also enabled relays of messengers on horseback to provide a fast, efficient postal service. Herodotus was so impressed by these messengers that he wrote of them, "Neither snow, nor rain, nor heat, nor gloom of night stays these couriers from the swift completion of their appointed rounds."

See also:

The Assyrians (volume 2, page 208) • The Peloponnesian War (volume 3, page 368)

This statue of a griffin is located at Persepolis, the capital of the Persian Empire.

THE DARK AGE AND GREEK EXPANSION

After the fall of the Mycenaean civilization, Greece entered a period that is now known as the Dark Age. Gradually, however, Greece emerged from this era, and exiles from the country founded colonies all around the Mediterranean region.

By the mid-13th century BCE, the cities and palaces of mainland Greece were feeling under threat. New construction surrounded many of the cities with strong fortified walls, and measures were taken to protect underground water supplies, suggesting that imminent invasion was feared. This fear seems not to have been misplaced. By the end of the century, all the palaces had been burned, and the once great Mycenaean civilization was in terminal decline.

The cause of this collapse was a vast influx of Dorian peoples from central Asia. These aggressive tribesmen swept down mainland Greece from the north, traveling in ox-drawn covered wagons and inspiring terror with their horned helmets. By 1100 BCE, all the main Mycenaean centers had fallen to these invaders, and for the next few centuries, Greece entered what is called the Dark Age, about which very little is known.

An age of poverty

Archaeological excavations suggest that Greece became impoverished and partially depopulated in the turbulent period following the collapse of the Mycenaean culture. The arrival of the Dorians resulted in a change in the spoken dialect and in iron being used in preference to bronze, but the number and size of both settlements and burial grounds declined sharply, while the primitive style of buildings and earthenware show that the people lived in great poverty. The complete disappearance of the complex society once centered on the palaces meant that writing skills were also lost. The social organization seems to have broken down into small communities, each led by a *basileus*. In the palace hierarchy, this title had been used for a subordinate figure, but in the Dark Age, the title referred to a powerful chieftain who held independent authority.

It seems that the population increased again in the ninth century BCE, possibly due to a reduction in mortality or an increase in migration. What is certain is that the Greeks began to migrate from the mainland around this time, some to Cyprus, Crete, and the Aegean islands, others to Anatolia. Over the course of the ninth century, representatives of three main dialect groups (see box, page 250) settled in much of the coastal region of Anatolia and on the islands off this coast. Those speaking the Aeolic dialect settled on the island of Lesbos and in the region from north of the Dardanelles on the northwest coast of Anatolia down to

The Temple of Hera on the island of Samos in the Aegean Sea. Samos was settled by Ionians during the Dark Age and later became an important trading center.

246

Smyrna. Ionians settled on the central part of the coast from Smyrna to Miletus and on the islands of Chios and Samos. Dorians settled in the southern part from Halicarnassus down to the southernmost coast and on the islands of Rhodes and Cos. Some of the many settlements created on these islands and in the coastal regions developed into important cities—in particular, the 12 Ionian settlements called the *dodeca poleis* (the 12 cities).

The migration to the various islands and to Anatolia stimulated further exploration, and the former trading routes with the east were soon restored. Linking large parts of the Mediterranean world with the Greek world, these routes had declined during the Dark Age but had never been completely severed. Toward the end of the ninth century BCE, Greek seafarers could once again be found in the harbors of northern Syria and Phoenicia.

This terra-cotta figurine, known as the Lefkandi Centaur, was found on the island of Euboea. The figurine dates to the 10th century BCE and is a rare relic from the Dark Age.

The Archaic period

The restoration of trade with the east had momentous results for the Greeks. The Greek world emerged from its temporary isolation and began to experience such great changes that a new era is defined as beginning around 750 BCE. The new world that was developing bore little resemblance to the old Bronze Age civilization. Historians call this new era the Archaic period.

During the Archaic period, increased contact with the east brought the Greeks new ideas regarding pottery, sculpture, architecture, mythology, religion, and the use of iron and bronze. Most important of all was the reintroduction of writing, this time using an alphabet derived from Phoenician examples (see box, page 252). It is not clear exactly when the Greeks started to adapt the Semitic alphabet to their own needs, but the oldest inscriptions using the new alphabet date from the second half of the eighth century BCE. After that, the use of the alphabet spread rapidly, making it possible to record the *Iliad* and the *Odyssey*;

THE GREEK WORLD IN THE DARK AGE

Olbia
Tyras
Black Sea
Phasis
THRACE
Sinope
ANATOLIA
MACEDON
Thasos
Dardanelles
LYDIA
Pithekoussai
Aegean Sea
GREECE
LESBOS
CHIOS
Smyrna
ATTICA
Thebes
SAMOS
Corinth
EVVOIA
Miletus
Athens
Halicarnassus
Mylai
ARCADIA
Argos
COS
Side
Soloi
SICILY
Sparta
RHODES
CYPRUS
ASSYRIA
CRETE
Mediterranean Sea
Cyrene
EGYPT
Memphis

these two epics were almost certainly first composed in the oral tradition.

The beginning of the Archaic period also saw the emergence of the polis (plural: poleis), which was an autonomous political unit covering a small territory, usually averaging between 50 and 100 square miles (260 km²), with a population of between 2,500 and 4,500. Some poleis were larger than this, particularly those of Sparta, Argos, Corinth, Athens, and Thebes. There were also some very small units covering a territory of no more than 15 square miles (39 km²) and having a population of only around 250. However large or small, each polis had at least one settlement that was called a city (also, confusingly, called a polis), no matter how small or unlike a city it actually was.

Each polis was completely independent. In theory, all the freemen who were its citizens organized the political affairs of the polis (from which the term *politics* is derived) in community assemblies, but in fact, much of the real power rested with the aristocracy. The basileus, who in the Dark Age had ruled as a king, was replaced in most cases by magistrates who were elected annually from the ranks of the nobles. These aristocrats owed their dominant position to a combination of

KEY

The Greek world in 900 BCE

Coast under Greek influence by around 500 BCE

249

THE GREEK DIALECT GROUPS

Dialect was a significant factor in the Greek migrations of the ninth century BCE because people tended to settle into linguistic groups. Doric was the dialect of northwest Greece. It was also spoken along the west of Greece and on the islands of Crete, Cos, and Rhodes as a result of Dorian conquests between 1200 and 1000 BCE. Doric spread to Anatolia as Dorian speakers settled there in the ninth century BCE.

The non-Doric dialects were Ionic, Aeolic, and Arcado-Cyprian. Ionic was the language of Attica and the island of Evvoia, while Aeolic was spoken in the northeast and center of mainland Greece. Arcado-Cyprian, the dialect spoken in Arcadia on the Peloponnese and on Cyprus, is closely related to Mycenaean Greek, in which the Linear B inscriptions were written. This affinity to Linear B may be due to the fact that there was little migrant influence in the wild and rugged Arcadian region and that Cyprus had served as a haven for refugees from the mainland during the time of the invasions.

The greatest differences were those between the Dorians and the Ionians, two groups who spoke different tongues, had different customs and religious practices, and who each built up a position of power. These differences led to the Peloponnesian War (431–404 BCE).

This portrait from a Roman mosaic is believed to depict the poetess Sappho, who wrote in the Aeolic dialect.

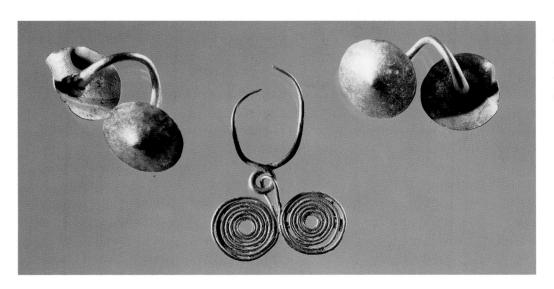

These gold earrings were found at Lefkandi on Euboea and date to the mid-ninth century BCE.

power and wealth, which, in the early Archaic period, was often expressed in the number of horses one owned. After 700 BCE, the possession of bronze armor was another indicator of status.

Colonization

The emergence of the poleis took place during a time of rapid population growth. This rise in population led to the conquest of sparsely populated regions and to armed conflicts between neighboring poleis in attempts to expand their territories. The rise also encouraged further emigration of Greeks from the mainland. In the eighth century BCE, Sparta subjected the region of Laconia and began the conquest of neighboring Messenia. Argos extended its power over the Argolis region, while Athens united the peninsula of Attica into one polis. The emigration of many Greeks to settlements on the Mediterranean and Black Sea coasts led to what is called the Archaic colonization.

Developments such as colonization and the subsequent flourishing of trade, the growing contact between the various poleis, and the use of writing to record the laws and decrees of a polis community all had an influence on the relations between the many small states of the Greek world. Within the poleis, social relations were changing as some citizens became a great deal richer than others. An elite of aristocrats and wealthy citizens emerged as a result of trading with the east. In several poleis, these small groups of aristocrats managed to seize control and end the community assemblies, thereby undermining the fundamental principle of the poleis. As the majority of the citizens still had to work to survive, they were often forced into a

This sixth-century-BCE Greek vase painting shows Ajax carrying the body of Achilles. The tales of Homer were not written down until the Archaic period.

THE GREEK ALPHABETS

The word *alphabet* comes from the first two letters of the Greek alphabet—alpha and beta—and denotes a writing system in which a single character (grapheme) represents a single sound (phoneme). Non-alphabetic systems of writing use signs that represent whole words or syllables. The Mesopotamian cuneiform system used a combination of word and syllable signs, while Egyptian hieroglyphs used signs that represented words together with signs that represented a group of consonants or a single consonant. Around 1500 BCE, elements of the Egyptian hieroglyphic script were adapted to create a script in which each individual sound of a language (apart from vowel sounds) was represented by a single symbol—that is, an alphabet. This adaptation took place somewhere in the Syro-Palestinian region, and the inventors of the new script spoke a Semitic language.

The new alphabetic script soon took on different forms as its use spread among different peoples over the course of the following centuries. One script developed in the 14th and 13th centuries BCE in the city of Ugarit on the coast of Syria consisted of a cuneiform (wedge-shaped) alphabet of 30 characters. One of the principal variants was the Northwest Semitic alphabet, from which nearly all alphabetic scripts in use today are ultimately descended. A short version, using 22 letters, was being used to write the Phoenician language from the 11th century BCE, and from Phoenicia it spread to neighboring regions in the Middle East.

The Greeks adopted this short Phoenician alphabet in the eighth century BCE and modified it by adding two or more consonant symbols. They also began to use some of the symbols to represent vowel sounds. For a time, they experimented with writing from left to right and from right to left, but by around 500 BCE, they settled on left to right. As the Greek alphabet spread, it was adopted and modified by various Mediterranean peoples, including the Etruscans, the Umbrians, the Oscans, and the Romans. The last were to be the most influential, since the Roman alphabet, used to write Latin, was subsequently to be used by all the languages of western Europe.

This tablet found on the island of Pylos is inscribed with Linear B script. The Greeks later adopted the Phoenician alphabet.

The Temple of Ceres at Paestum. Paestum, a Greek colony in southern Italy, was founded around the beginning of the seventh century BCE.

dependent relationship with rich land-holders. Many of the poorer citizens were exploited, and if they got into debt, they could be sold into slavery.

In Sparta, attempts were made to resolve the internal tensions by making all citizens equal, at the expense of an underprivileged group that was excluded from citizenship and left with no rights at all. In Athens and Corinth, rivalry between aristocrats led to internal polit-ical conflict. In some cases, an aristocrat would succeed in seizing absolute power and set himself up as an all-powerful sov-ereign—this was a new kind of monarch that the Greeks called a *tyrannis* (tyrant).

After the horrors of the Dark Age, the Archaic period saw the Greeks emerging into an era of prosperity that in turn led to a flowering of new ideas and artistic achievement. The spread of writing had a profound effect on law and government. Because the results of law suits could now be recorded, leading to the estab-lishment of legal codes, any citizen could appeal against an arbitrary ruling by a corrupt magistrate and cite legal prece-dent to uphold the appeal. This change led to more rational government and the rule of law.

Greek expansion

The period of Greek overseas settlement that began in the middle of the eighth century BCE lasted for more than 200 years. During that time, Greeks founded dozens of settlements on the fringes of the Aegean, Mediterranean, and Black seas. The impetus behind this colonizing movement may have originally been trade, but the settlements soon became new, independent states. These colonies (not a strictly accurate term for the settlements) inherited various social and political aspects—such as religious cults, political organizations, and spoken dialect—from their metropolis (parent city), but the colonies themselves were completely independent entities.

An overseas polis often started as a trading post (*emporion*), which then developed into a settlement as colonists followed. Trade was certainly the moti-vating factor in some of the very early Greek colonies, such as Al Mina in Syria and Pithekoussai in Italy. Greek traders were looking to buy iron ore, silver, and slaves, while offering wine and olive oil in return. A trading post that turned into a colony was called an *apoikia*, meaning a "settlement elsewhere." Most *apoikiai* started with no more than one or two hundred people, to be joined by other colonists at a later stage. The new colony would always hold its parent metropolis in esteem and would preserve the religious customs of the parent city despite any political differences. The metropolis and satellite polis would send official envoys to each other's religious festivals, and the special relationship was sometimes demonstrated by the provision of military aid by the parent to the colony. For example, Corinth helped the city of Syracuse to fight the Athenians during the Peloponnesian War, because Syracuse was Corinth's colony.

The spread of settlements

Colonies fanned out in all directions from the Greek mainland. Some of the earliest settlements were on Sicily and in southern Italy, where the colonists were attracted by the good harbors and fertile land to support farming. The Greek presence there became so dominant that the area was called Magna Grecia (Great Greece). In the fifth century BCE, Syracuse on Sicily became the most highly populated of all Greek cities. Other new settlements were situated on the Aegean islands along the northern coast of the Aegean Sea; on the northern coast of Anatolia along the Hellespont and the Bosporus; around the Black Sea; on the north African coast in Cyrenaica (present-day Libya); and on the south coast of France and the northeastern coast of Spain.

The Greek colonists avoided areas where other peoples had a significant presence. These areas included the eastern coast of the Mediterranean, which was already well occupied, and the northeast African coast, which was largely avoided because of the dominance of Egypt in the area. The African coast to

The Sicilian town of Syracuse, the site of this ancient Greek theater, was settled by exiles from Corinth in the eighth century BCE.

Elea, the ruins of which are shown here, was a Greek colony on the mainland of Italy. The colony was founded in the sixth century BCE.

the west of Cyrenaica was entirely in the hands of the Phoenicians, as was the western part of Sicily, the whole of Sardinia, most of the smaller islands in the western Mediterranean, and a large part of the Spanish coast.

Adventurous colonists

Why the Greek colonists wanted to leave the mother country is not completely clear. The theory that they were escaping overpopulation on the mainland has been largely discredited, but they may have been fleeing from an unsatisfactory political situation at home, or seeking land of their own, or simply searching for adventure. When a group of emigrants boarded a ship or—as some sources imply—were taken aboard forcibly, the people were already well prepared for their enterprise. They knew where they

wanted to go and had consulted an oracle before setting out to ensure a favorable outcome to the voyage. At least, that is what they were supposed to do. Colonies that did not possess the text of an oracle, or that could not point out the tomb of an original founder, often produced forgeries in order to ensure their standing.

When the immigrants disembarked at their destination, the first thing they did was to drive away the native population, if there was one. It is not known whether it was common practice to subdue the original inhabitants and bind them in servitude to the Greeks, but this undoubtedly happened from time to time. The second task was to find a site where the new city could be built and divide the surrounding land equally among the colonists. This practice served

A POET FARMER

One poet who seems to mark the transition between the heroic epic poetry of Homer and the more practical, personal work of writers such as Archilochus is Hesiod, a farmer who lived in Boeotia around 700 BCE. Whereas the two epic poems of Homer, the *Iliad* and the *Odyssey*, portrayed a legendary time of superheroes who fought with formidable foes and overcame huge obstacles with the help of the gods, Hesiod's poetry dealt with his own world. Although his poetry retained the traditional epic form, the content of it was novel. Hesiod saw the world as a chaotic place where the individual was on his own in trying to achieve good relations with the gods and his fellow men. Hesiod sometimes featured himself in his poems, and in his "Contest between Homer and Hesiod," he awards the prize to himself, claiming that he stands for peace and plowshares rather than swords and slaughter.

to create an aristocracy of the earliest settlers, who had first choice of land and became premier citizens. Immigrants who arrived later would probably be granted civil rights and a small piece of land, but they would almost certainly be accorded a subordinate position in the new society. This practice explains the existence of the extensive elite groups that occupied the aristocratic councils in many of the colonies. It is not clear whether women accompanied the original colonists. They may have been sent for later, or they may have been sought— or abducted—from neighboring regions.

When a trading post developed into a more permanent community, it usually took the form of an agricultural settlement. No matter how much trading took place, arable land was of prime importance, and most Greek colonies were founded in regions with good agricultural land. Some commentators have deduced from this pattern that Archaic colonization was motivated by a shortage of land in the homeland. While many of the colonists were probably driven to emigrate for economic reasons, this motivation would not have applied to the aristocratic and wealthier colonists who may have left a parent city for political reasons.

Exporting a culture

The natural consequence of Greek colonization was not only a migration of people but a migration of their whole culture, including their technological skills, their customs, their religion, and their concepts and attitudes. The Greeks took with them everything, from specific agricultural methods and crops like the olive and grape to architectural and building skills and an entire hierarchy of gods. This export of culture from the Aegean region to, particularly, the Italian region was to have a profound effect on European history. The colonies of "Great Greece" were to form a bridge between east and west, just as the Mycenaeans and the Phoenicians had done previously.

A good example of this influence can be seen in the colony at Pithekoussai on Ischia, an Italian island in the Bay of Naples. Excavations carried out there since the mid-20th century CE have established that this settlement was founded by colonists from the Aegean island of Evvoia. Certainly not a typical colony, Pithekoussai was a very early settlement of the eighth century BCE and was located right on the northern frontier of what was later to become the Greek world. The colony appears to have started as an *emporion* and subsequently developed into an *apoikia*. Greek settlements functioned as a corridor through which eastern influences reached the Iron Age cultures of Italy and beyond, stimulating major changes. In the seventh and sixth centuries BCE, a Mediterranean urban culture began to take root in the Etruscan region of central Italy.

In addition to generating changes in the occupied regions, the Greek colonies also stimulated developments in the motherland. The existence of strong and independent colonies overseas boosted trade considerably. Grain from Sicily and southern Russia was brought to mainland Greece, while wine, bronze plate, and high-quality pottery were the main commodities sent from the motherland to the colonies. The colonial Greeks then often sold on these products to indigenous rulers in the hinterland.

Finds of pottery and other artifacts in various locations have enabled archaeologists to trace trade movements and map the contacts between Greeks and non-Greeks. It has been discovered, for instance, that Carthaginian and Greek traders supplied bronze products, pottery, wine, and other luxury articles via intermediaries to chieftains who lived in remote inland parts of western and central Europe. These goods were exchanged for silver, tin, or slaves. The Celtic chiefs of Gaul were among those who prospered from trade with the Greeks, as evidenced by the number of luxury Greek items found in their burial chambers. One particular example was a Greek bronze krater (a vessel for mixing wine with water) that was found in the tomb of a ruler in Vix in the Seine valley.

Poetry of the colonies

Besides bringing Greek architecture, sculpture, and art to the new settlements, the colonists also imported Greek poetry. One of these colonial poets was Archilochus, who, in the seventh century BCE, left his birthplace on the island of Paros to go to Thasos (an island off the Thracian coast), where the inhabitants of Paros were founding a colony.

Archilochus was one of the first Greek lyric poets. Unlike the epic poems of Homer, Archilocus's work describes everyday life and the poet's personal feel-

ings about the world around him. Often sarcastic in tone, the poems convey strong feelings about his new life abroad.

Joining an early emigrant voyage to Thasos, Archilochus experienced first-hand the rigors of life on the frontier at that time. The settlement was under constant threat from Thracian tribesmen, and the settlers found life hard. Archilochus himself lamented his stay in the "triply dreadful city of Thasos," where, as he put it, "the dregs of the entire Greek nation" came together to fight "the Thracian dogs." Archilochus's view of Thasos gives a fascinating glimpse into the mind of the Greek colonist, with his idealistic view of the paradise over the horizon.

This bust depicts the Greek poet Hesiod, who lived in the eighth century BCE.

See also:

Mycenae and Troy (volume 2, page 182) • The Phoenicians (volume 2, page 196)

SPARTA AND ATHENS

The rivalry of the two city-states Sparta and Athens formed an important part of the history of ancient Greece. Both cities underwent changes in their political structure from the eighth century BCE onward.

The eighth century BCE saw the emergence in Greece of the polis (plural: poleis), the city-state. Two city-states that had very different histories and characteristics were Sparta and Athens.

Sparta

The polis of Sparta had its origins in several small settlements on the Eurotas Plain in Laconia in the southern part of the Peloponnese. In the 10th century BCE, the Eurotas Plain was invaded by warriors who spoke the Doric dialect. Subduing the native population, the invaders moved into several villages grouped near the hills in the center of the plain and formed the settlement that was to become Sparta. Over the next two centuries, the Spartans, as they came to be called, developed a regime that differed considerably from that of other Greek city-states. The highest level of the social hierarchy of this new polis consisted of the conquering warriors—the Spartans—who were led by two kings. The conquered people consisted of helots, or serfs, and *perioikoi*, who were neighboring freemen who recognized the authority of the Spartan kings.

By the eighth century BCE, Sparta had expanded to such an extent that there was not sufficient land in Laconia to provide a reasonable living for all the warriors of the growing population. On the other side of the Taygetus Mountains lay the highly fertile region of Messenia. After a lengthy war, the Spartans succeeded in conquering Messenia toward the end of the eighth century. From that time onward, the original settlement on the Eurotas Plain remained the heart of the state, while Messenia was regarded as occupied territory.

The Messenians found the regime under the Spartans so oppressive that they revolted in the seventh century BCE; the rising was only finally put down after decades of strife. During this period, the Spartan poet Tyrtaeus wrote battle songs, and his verses constitute the oldest written record of Sparta's history. In one song, Tyrtaeus describes the rewards that the conquerors would enjoy when all the Messenians were made into helots: "Like heavily laden donkeys, they will be forced by hard means to hand over to their masters half of what they harvest in their fields." This prophecy was soon to be fulfilled.

The helots

By the mid-seventh century BCE, Sparta had finally subdued the Messenians and was the largest of all the Greek city-states. Sparta had an immense labor force of helots to work its fertile lands, making it also one of the most prosperous city-states. The helots functioned as serfs,

This statue is a copy of the Athena Promachos, a giant statue of the goddess Athena that stood in Athens. The deity was the city's patron, and the original statue was destroyed in the 13th century CE.

carrying out all the agricultural work while their Spartan masters concentrated on military matters. In time of war, helots were used to row the long galleys or as low-ranking soldiers in the field. They had no civil rights, but in contrast to slaves, helots could not be owned by individual Spartans.

Best described as "slaves of the state," the helots belonged to particular plots of land and could not be bought and sold individually. When land was allocated to a Spartan citizen, it came complete with helots, and he was not allowed to sell or release them. The state determined the percentage of the harvest that the helots had to hand over to their masters. The helots were allowed to keep the remainder of the food for themselves.

There were a few legal ways for a helot to secure freedom. A Spartan father could adopt any children he had by a helot mother, making the children Spartan citizens. From the fifth century BCE onward, helots could earn the status of freeman by fighting with the Spartans as full-fledged soldiers in wartime. In neither case did the helot acquire full Spartan civil rights.

Although they were essential for the agricultural economy, helots were by no means always well treated. Spartan citizens were vastly outnumbered by helots and lived in constant fear of an uprising. Consequently, the Spartans attempted to keep the helots firmly under control by systematic humiliation and intimidation. This treatment included the *krypteia*—a kind of secret police in which young Spartans were enrolled to hunt and kill helots in the wilderness. This practice seems to have been a sort of initiation ritual that involved a period of isolation followed by the killing of an "enemy." However, it is probable that only a few helots were murdered in this way; a large-scale culling of the workforce would have had serious negative economic implications.

Perioikoi

The other people who were not entitled to Spartan civil rights were the *perioikoi*—usually translated as neighbors or out-dwellers. These people were

Greek ruins in the Messenia region, which was conquered by Sparta in the eighth century BCE.

SPARTA, ATHENS, AND THEIR RIVALS

freemen descended from the pre-Dorian inhabitants of the region and lived on the outskirts of the polis. Most of the *perioikoi* were farmers, and although they had no political rights within the Spartan state, their communities were internally autonomous. In peacetime, Sparta had little interest in the settlements, but in times of war, the settlements were expected to supply soldiers.

Spartan males were trained from a young age to become soldiers and were banned from engaging in trade or crafts. For this reason, it was the *perioikoi* who formed the class of traders and craftsmen that exported iron ore, limestone for building, bronze figurines, and painted pottery.

Lycurgus and the constitution

After the final subjugation of the Messenians, a number of changes took place in Spartan society. While the basic administrative and social structure that had existed since the conquest of Laconia continued, it was adapted and systematized in the late seventh and early sixth centuries BCE. These reforms have

Two Greek wrestlers prepare to fight in this relief sculpture. In ancient Sparta, sports such as wrestling were considered an important part of military training.

traditionally been attributed to the great lawgiver Lycurgus, although it is not clear whether any such man ever existed. It is more probable that the reformed constitution was not the work of one man, but rather the result of an evolutionary process. However it was arrived at, the constitution of the revised state is generally referred to as the Lycurgan Constitution, to distinguish it from the earlier society.

Under the Lycurgan Constitution, the joint rule of two kings continued. However, apart from their joint command of the army, most of their functions were purely honorary. The real power lay not with the kings but with three other institutions: the assembly, the council of elders, and the magistrates.

The public assembly, called the *apella*, was an assembly of adult warriors with Spartan civil rights. This assembly had the power to vote on motions presented by the council of elders (the *gerousia*) but could not propose its own motions. Nor could the assembly make amendments to motions laid before it. Voting took place by means of booing or cheering, the outcome being determined by the group that made the most noise.

The most powerful of the governing bodies was the *gerousia*, which consisted of 28 men all aged 60 and above. Each member was either related to one of the kings or came from an aristocratic family, and they were all elected for life. The *gerousia* prepared motions to be debated in the assembly and served as a Supreme Court, with authority to try even the kings if it seemed they had fallen short of their duties.

When motions were voted on in the assembly, the volume of noise was judged by the five *ephors* (overseers), the highest magistrates in the polis. These officials, in whom ultimate authority lay, were elected annually by the assembly and constituted the actual government of Sparta, supervising the entire range of state affairs. The *ephors* held regular meetings with the *gerousia*, influencing the choice of items to be debated at the assembly, and had monthly meetings with the two kings, at which the kings pledged themselves to observe the laws. In return, the *ephors* promised to support the kings, provided the kings did indeed observe the laws. If the kings and the *ephors* had disagreements, the *ephors*, who had the last word, could charge the kings with misconduct, fine them, dethrone them, and even send them into exile.

Military training

In Lycurgan Sparta, the army was of paramount importance, and all Spartan boys had to undergo rigorous training from a very early age for a military life. At birth, infants were inspected by state officials, and any infants deemed to be defective were exposed on the mountains and left to die. At the age of seven, boys were taken from their homes and brought up in "packs," which were supervised by older boys. When they were twelve, the boys were placed in barracks, where they lived on a basic diet of porridge enriched with bits of pork. Their education was primarily physical, consisting mostly of athletics and combat sports practiced naked in all weathers outdoors. Throughout, the emphasis was on learning to obey orders without hesitation and to endure hardships.

At age 20, the warrior graduated and was allotted a plot of land that would provide food to feed himself and his family. He joined a *sussitia* (one of the military messes) to which he would belong

This 19th-century-CE engraving depicts the Spartan lawgiver Lycurgus, who is credited with transforming Sparta's political structure.

for the rest of his life, and he became eligible to vote in the assembly. Spartan males were conditioned to relate primarily to other men. Indeed, part of their youthful training involved being paired with another older boy in what was almost certainly a sexual relationship.

Even when a man and a woman married, they lived in separate male and female quarters, although they were allowed to share a room at night. Marriage was endorsed by the state, since it was necessary to raise another generation of warriors and mothers of warriors. Since it was deemed important that women should be healthy to bear healthy children, great attention was devoted to the physical education of girls. The girls participated—naked, to the amazement of other Greeks—along with boys in the athletics program until the age of 18. To ensure that girls would not embark on pregnancy too young, the marriageable age for girls in Sparta was higher than elsewhere in Greece.

An austere life

From the sixth century BCE, Spartan society became increasingly austere and rigid. Everything was focused on the maintenance of a powerful army, and Sparta became an introverted community where change was seen as undesirable and strangers were not welcome. The Spartan ideology was rooted in the primacy of the state over the needs of the individual. Even today, the word *Spartan* carries a connotation of strict austerity in all aspects of lifestyle.

The settlement of Sparta itself was no more than a collection of villages, not worthy of being called a city. With the exception of a few temples, there were no stone buildings, only mud huts. The art of poetry, which had flourished in the seventh century, died away, and the once famous bronze and pottery work of Laconia also declined.

Music and dance remained important in the religious life of Sparta, but here too creativity was lacking. Only in the military field did Sparta play a prominent role in Greece. During the Persian Wars, Sparta assumed the military leadership almost automatically, and the heroic death of King Leonidas and his followers in the pass of Thermopylae in 480 BCE reinforced Sparta's claim to this leadership.

However, there were some in the ancient world who admired Sparta not only for its military strength, but also for its fine example of virtue, honesty, austerity, and fidelity. The philosopher Plato declared that Sparta came closest to his concept of the ideal state. Many historians, however, would argue that Sparta's rival, Athens, would have a greater claim to the title.

Athens

The city-state of Athens consisted of the city of Athens and the region surrounding it—the Attic Peninsula (generally called Attica) on the east coast of mainland Greece. Attica is largely mountainous and dry, but it does have a number of reasonably fertile plains. It is separated from central Greece and the Corinthian isthmus by virtually impassable mountains, but it is enclosed by sea on two sides and has good natural harbors. These harbors allowed the people of Attica to trade by sea and, when necessary, set out by sea for distant lands.

Athens originated as a Mycenaean settlement on and around the Acropolis, a rocky outcrop that lies in the middle of the largest plain of Attica. Legend has it that during the Mycenaean period the Athenian king Theseus united 12 Attican villages into one polis, but whether this has any basis in historical fact is not known. It can, however, be established that the Mycenaean fortress on the Acropolis was never destroyed and that Athens was continuously inhabited from

No traces of the ancient city remain on the plains of Sparta. The ruins in the foreground date from a much later period (the 13th to 15th century CE).

THE HOPLITE

From around the eight century BCE onward, the key component of the armies of ancient Greece was the hoplite. The hoplite was a heavily armed footsoldier who fought in close formation. The hoplite took his name from the word *hoplon*, meaning a piece of armor. His main weapon was a spear that was around 9 feet (2.7 m) long. He would also carry a short sword for stabbing his enemies at close quarters.

By the fifth century BCE, the hoplite's armor would consist of a large circular shield known as an *aspis*, a breastplate, a pair of greaves (shin protectors), and a helmet. There were various styles of helmet, but one of the most common was the Corinthian, which protected both the bridge of the nose and the cheeks. Early Corinthian helmets also covered the ears, but this design made hearing difficult. Because soldiers needed to hear instructions in the heat of battle, later variations had holes cut out for the ears. In illustrations on Greek vases, helmets are usually topped by a magnificent crest, but historians believe that many helmets did without such decorations. In total, the armor could weigh up to 60 pounds (27 kg), so hoplites needed to be very strong.

In battle, the hoplites fought by marching forward in a dense formation several rows deep. The left-hand side of each soldier's shield covered the right-hand side of the soldier next to him. The spears of the soldiers further back would go over the shoulders of the troops in front of them, presenting the enemy with a wall of spears. Once the two sides engaged, the battle would often degenerate into a brutal pushing contest. As soon as the formation of one side broke apart, the battle was effectively over.

The hoplites were not professional soldiers, but rather an army of citizens who took up arms when the need arose. Because armor was fairly expensive, the hoplites came from the wealthier ranks of society. In the case of most cities, the hoplites had jobs and farms to go back to, so campaigning seasons were short.

The most fearsome hoplites were those from Sparta. Although they were not professional soldiers, in the sense of being a paid, standing army, the fact that all Spartan men trained in military skills from birth meant that Spartan hoplites were fitter, more organized, and more disciplined than those from other cities.

This relief from the fifth century BCE depicts two hoplites following a chariot and carrying the typical round shield (aspis) *and long spear.*

the late Helladic period, through the Dark Age, to the Archaic period. There is therefore a grain of truth in the claim by the Athenians that they were the original indigenous Greeks whose domain had never been conquered by invaders.

Social groups

As far as its social and political structure was concerned, Athens followed the pattern of many of the other Greek city-states. There were three distinct social groups. Dominating the others were the *hippei*—horsemen or knights. These men were the aristocrats who owned the most land, which was usually worked by their tenants. In the second rank were the *zeugitai*, men who owned a *zeugos* or yoke for a pair of oxen. These men were farmers who owned enough land to be economically independent. Below both of these groups were the *thetes*, who were small farmers and day laborers. In principle, all these groups, from the aristocrats to the landless, were Athenian citizens. This situation was fairly unusual, because in many city-states, land ownership and civil rights were linked.

From the seventh century BCE, or perhaps earlier, Athens had a board of nine magistrates, called the *archons*, who were elected annually. These *archons* were always drawn from the ranks of the aristocracy. Ex-*archons* became members of the *areopagus*, a council named after the place where it convened, the Areos Pagos, or hill of the god Ares.

Social tension

Athens experienced enormous social tension in the seventh century BCE. Poor small farmers frequently lost their land to richer landholders and were subsequently forced to rent farmland at an exorbitant rate—one sixth of the yield, which was a high price to pay in the relatively dry and infertile Attica region. Anyone who could not pay the rent was declared a debtor, and creditors were merciless in enforcing their claims against debtors. People who could not pay were often sold into slavery, together with their wives

A shoemaker goes about his daily work in this illustration from a Greek vase.

and children. This conflicted greatly with the notion that all Athenians had equal rights in the polis. Growing discontent brought with it the danger of civil unrest, and the constant competition among the aristocrats led to the fear that one of them might take advantage of the situation and seize power for himself.

Solon

One way to deal with the social tension was to reform the law. At the beginning of the sixth century BCE, an aristocrat named Solon, who had been a distinguished general, was appointed chief *archon* with special powers to revise the law and act as an arbitrator to avoid the threat of civil war. Solon was to go down in Greek history as an outstanding example of a wise lawgiver, and many institutions from a later period were also attributed to him.

One of Solon's' first decisions was to invite a number of emigrants and exiles to return to Athens. Some of these people had been banished from the country for political reasons, while others had fled due to the huge burden of debt incurred as tenant farmers. To enable people in the latter group to return, Solon negotiated the cancellation of all their debts. He also abolished debt slavery, making it impossible for someone to guarantee a debt with his own person. All the debt slaves who could be traced had their freedoms purchased for them.

Besides being a economic reformer, Solon was also a poet. He recorded his reforms in the following verses: "I gave Athens, divine city, back its sons; men who were sold either lawfully or unlawfully; men who were driven from their native country by poverty; vagrants who had almost forgotten how to speak their own language. I did this by using the laws and powers given to me."

It is not clear whether anything was done to prevent a new buildup of debts.

Poor Athenians probably had to work as agricultural laborers from then on, while some people may have found work in the newly emerging industries.

Political changes

In addition to his efforts in the economic field, Solon was active in political reform. He decreed that all free citizens of Attica be allowed to vote in the public assembly, the *ecclesia*. Other political rights were linked to a division of the citizens into classes. These classes were defined by Solon according to a new criterion based solely on property; previously, birth had been the most important factor. The classification was based on annual income expressed in terms of quantities of grain, and there were four groups. In addition to the *thetes*, *zeugitai*, and *hippeis*, a new group was formed.

This sculpture is believed to depict Solon, one of the most important Athenian statesmen of the sixth century BCE.

267

ATHENIAN WOMEN

Unlike the women of Sparta, women in Athens had a very low status. Although nominally Athenian citizens, the women were not allowed to vote or to attend the assembly, and their ability to inherit property was very limited.

Most Athenian women were virtually confined to the home, where they spent their days in domestic duties such as looking after the children, spinning and weaving to make clothes for the family, and cleaning. Upper-class women had slaves to perform these duties and needed only to oversee the work. A woman was always in the guardianship of a man, either her husband, her father, or her brother. Only lower-class women worked—perhaps cleaning streets or participating in a menial trade.

Even in the home, women were segregated from the affairs of men and spent most of their time in the women's quarters, where men seldom went. Athenian society was very much a man's society,

and a woman's main role was to give birth, particularly to male infants. Fathers had the right to reject an infant of the wrong sex, and it seems that infanticide was a regular occurrence. A girl was raised in the women's quarters and might see her father only rarely. When she was seven, she might attend school to learn to read and write, and by the time she was 12 or 14, she was considered ready for marriage.

A woman's life expectancy was 36 years, less than that of a man, which was probably because, marrying young, women were worn out by childbearing. However, many women did survive their husbands, who might have been considerably older. If a widow remarried, her inheritance became the property of her new husband.

This painting from the 19th century CE depicts Greek women drawing water from a well. Women in ancient Athens would have spent most of their time performing household tasks.

This new group, the *pentakosiomedimnoi* (five hundred medimners), comprised men with an annual income of more than 500 medimnoi (roughly 1,500 cubic feet or 420 hectoliters) of grain, or the equivalent. This new class was a group of the superrich (distinct from the broader group of *hippeis*) who were granted the honor of performing duties connected with the guardianship of the temple of the goddess Athena, and only they and the *hippeis* could be elected to the position of *archon*.

All Athenians had the opportunity to appeal against decisions made by the *archons*. In order to facilitate this, Solon turned the public assembly into the highest court of justice. A separate "people's court" and a council of 400 members drawn from the upper three classes were also attributed to Solon, though they may have originated at a later date.

Solon's reforms did not please everybody. The rich and privileged had to make sacrifices, while the poorer people were disappointed that Solon had not redistributed enough land. However, his reforms did achieve their goal, which was to make social justice a cornerstone of the Athenian state. Solon described his reforms as follows: "I gave the people the necessary power, without giving them too much honor; and I took away the excess power from the nobility, without offending their noble feelings unnecessarily. In this way the people follow their leaders without the leaders holding the reins too tightly or too loosely."

Solon's measures temporarily endorsed the dominance of the aristocracy while allowing the lower classes to become more involved in politics. The new property criteria made social advancement easier—an important social change that meant it was no longer necessary to be descended from the nobility to enjoy upperclass privileges—high income was sufficient. Some time after Solon, the aristocratic structure was to be replaced by a timocratic structure—one in which political power was in proportion to property ownership.

See also:

The Peloponnesian War (volume 3, page 368)

The Acropolis lies at the heart of the city of Athens. From the very earliest days of the city, the Acropolis was the site of important temples.

TIME LINE

WESTERN ASIA AND SOUTHEASTERN EUROPE	REST OF THE WORLD
c. 8500 BCE Farmers first settle in future Assyrian heartland.	
c. 6500 BCE Farming communities established on Greek mainland.	**c. 6000 BCE** First farmers present in southern Asia.
c. 5000 BCE Semitic-speaking people move into southern Mesopotamia.	**c. 5000 BCE** Emergence of Yang-shao culture in China.
c. 3000 BCE People living in Aegean begin to make bronze by mixing copper and tin. Dawn of Minoan culture on Crete. Phoenicians begin to settle in what is now Syria, Lebanon, and Israel. First settlement appears at Troy. Semitic speakers begin to settle on eastern coast of Mediterranean.	**c. 2900 BCE** Single-grave people replace funnel-beaker people in northern Europe.
c. 2800 BCE Invaders with knowledge of metalwork arrive on Greek mainland. Beginning of Early Helladic I period.	**c. 2750 BCE** Early Dynastic period begins in Egypt.
c. 2600 BCE Early Helladic II period begins in Greece; sophisticated stone settlements built. Phoenicians trading with Egypt by this time.	**c. 2600 BCE** Earliest Indus Valley civilization develops.
	c. 2550 BCE Work begins on Great Pyramid of Giza.
c. 2100 BCE Migrants from central Asia arrive on Greek mainland to establish Minyan culture.	**c. 2047 BCE** Mentuhotep II reunites Egypt.

c. 3000 BCE

	WESTERN ASIA AND SOUTHEASTERN EUROPE		REST OF THE WORLD	
	c. 2000 BCE	First large palace complexes built at Knossos and Phaistos on Crete. Distinct Assyrian culture emerges in northern Mesopotamia. Forerunners of Hittites migrate to Anatolia from central Asia.	c. 1900 BCE	Metalworkers in British Isles start working with bronze.
c. 1800 BCE	c. 1800 BCE	Abraham, ancestor of Israelites, believed to have lived in Ur around this time. He leaves Ur to settle in Canaan.	c. 1800 BCE	Unetician culture reaches height of influence in central Europe.
	c. 1760 BCE	Old Assyrian Empire comes to end after Ashur conquered by Babylonians.	c. 1766 BCE	Shang dynasty begins rule of Yellow River Valley.
	c. 1700 BCE	Early Minoan palaces destroyed, either by invaders or by an earthquake; later rebuilt.		
	c. 1650 BCE	Labarnas makes Hattushash center of Hittite Empire and changes his name to Hattusilis.		
	c. 1600 BCE	Mycenae becomes major power on Greek mainland. Some Hebrew tribes migrate to Egypt around this time.		
	c. 1595 BCE	Hittite army under Mursilis I sacks Babylon but is destroyed on way back to Hattushash.	1550 BCE	Ascent of Ahmose to throne of Egypt marks beginning of New Kingdom.
	c. 1525 BCE	Kings based at Knossos reach height of power.		

WESTERN ASIA AND SOUTHEASTERN EUROPE		REST OF THE WORLD	
c. 1500 BCE	Traditional date given for eruption of volcano on Greek island of Thera.	**c. 1500 BCE**	Tumulus culture replaces Unetician culture in parts of Europe. Aryans enter India from central Asia. First Vedas composed.
c. 1450 BCE	Minoan civilization comes to end. Palaces burned down, possibly by Mycenaean invaders. Mycenaeans invade Crete, making Knossos administrative center. Fortress at Tiryns, Greece, built around this time.		
c. 1380 BCE	Suppiluliumas I expands Hittite Empire with campaign of conquest. Beginning of Hittite New Kingdom.	**1353 BCE**	Amenhotep IV becomes pharaoh in Egypt; later changes name to Akhenaton and introduces new religion based around worship of sun god Aton.
c. 1275 BCE	Battle of Kadesh between Hittites and Egyptians ends in stalemate. Tomb known as Treasury of Atreus built at Mycenae, Greece.		
c. 1250 BCE	Mycenaean era comes to end, possibly as result of invasion from the north. Troy VIIa, the Troy of Homer, destroyed. Shalmaneser I conquers Mitanni Empire to greatly expand area controlled by Assyrians. Influx of Dorian invaders from north heralds beginning of end of Mycenaean culture.		
c. 1200 BCE	Twelve Greek cities of Attica united by Theseus according to legend; form city-state of Athens.	**c. 1200 BCE**	Hallstatt culture emerges in present-day Austria; reaches height of influence between 800 and 500 BCE.

c. 1200 BCE

	WESTERN ASIA AND SOUTHEASTERN EUROPE	REST OF THE WORLD
	c. 1190 BCE Hittite New Kingdom collapses after attacks from Assyrians and Sea Peoples.	
	c. 1100 BCE Phoenicia establishes itself as dominant maritime power in Mediterranean. Greece enters Dark Age, period marked by poverty and depopulation.	**c. 1100 BCE** Iron Age begins in India.
		c. 1075 BCE New Kingdom comes to end in Egypt.
	c. 1050 BCE Troy VIIb destroyed; city abandoned for several centuries.	**c. 1050 BCE** Shang dynasty in China ousted by Zhou.
c. 1000 BCE	**c. 1000 BCE** King David makes Jerusalem capital of Kingdom of Israel.	**c. 1000 BCE** Caste system emerges in India. Lapita culture reaches Fiji. Nubia gains independence from Egypt. Copper industry flourishes in southern Congo.
	c. 950 BCE Construction begins on Temple of Jerusalem. Dorian invaders settle on Eurotas Plain in southern Greece; over next two centuries, they form city-state of Sparta.	**c. 900 BCE** First Brahmanas composed as glosses to Vedas.
	c. 883 BCE Assyrian Ashurnasirpal II begins campaigns of imperial expansion; also restores city of Nimrud.	
	c. 850 BCE Greeks begin migrations to Cyprus, Crete, Aegean islands, and Anatolia.	
	842 BCE Most Phoenician ports in Levant are absorbed into Assyrian Empire.	
	814 BCE Exiles from Tyre establish colony of Carthage; city goes on to become major power.	**753 BCE** Traditional date given for founding of Rome.

	WESTERN ASIA AND SOUTHEASTERN EUROPE		REST OF THE WORLD	
	c. 750 BCE	Beginning of Archaic period in Greece; developments include reintroduction of writing, increased trade, and emergence of poleis.		
	c. 729 BCE	Tiglath-pileser III unites Assyria and Babylonia under one rule.		
	c. 725 BCE	Spartans conquer neighboring region of Messenia; numerous revolts occur during following century.		
	c. 722 BCE	Northern Kingdom of Israel conquered by Assyrians.		
c. 700 BCE	c. 700 BCE	New style of poetry emerges in works of Greek writers Hesiod and Archilochus; poems contrast with epics of Homer.	c. 700 BCE	Scythians migrate into southern Russia from homeland in central Asia.
	c. 650 BCE	Spartan state reorganized; changes credited to lawgiver named Lycurgas.		
	c. 625 BCE	Social inequality leads to unrest in Athens.	c. 625 BCE	Large settlement forms between Palatine Hill and Capitoline Hill; gradually develops into city of Rome.
	c. 612 BCE	Nineveh falls to Babylonians; Assyrian Empire comes to end three years later.		
	c. 600 BCE	Athenian statesman Solon makes changes to Athenian society, including abolishing debt slavery.	c. 600 BCE	Iron Age arrives in northern Europe. City of Teotihuacán emerges in Mexico.

WESTERN ASIA AND SOUTHEASTERN EUROPE		REST OF THE WORLD	
c. 585 BCE	Jerusalem captured by Babylonians.	c. 563 BCE	Siddharta Gautama (later known as the Buddha) born.
559 BCE	Cyrus the Great ascends Persian throne; later conquers Medes to absorb lands into new Persian Empire.	551 BCE	Kongqiu (known in West as Confucius) born.
539 BCE	Phoenicia falls to Persian forces; Phoenician cities continue to flourish commercially.		
529 BCE	Persian king Cambyses II defeats Egyptian pharaoh at Pelusium; Egypt comes under Persian rule.	528 BCE	Siddharta becomes the Buddha.
521 BCE	Darius I takes Persian throne; reorganizes empire and embarks on campaigns of territorial expansion.		
490 BCE	Persian forces defeated by Greeks at Battle of Marathon.	c. 500 BCE	La Tène culture emerges in Switzerland; spreads over much of western Europe during following centuries. Zapotec people become powerful in southern Mexico.
479 BCE	Persians defeated by Greeks at Battle of Plataea.		
330 BCE	Phoenicia and Persian Empire conquered by Alexander the Great.	321 BCE	Mauryan period begins in Magadha, India.
85 BCE	Troy taken by Romans; city later becomes important trading port within Roman Empire.	82 BCE	Roman general Sulla declares himself dictator.
64 BCE	Phoenician city-states become part of Roman Empire.	63 BCE	Julius Caesar elected pontifex maximus.

529 BCE

GLOSSARY

Achaemenids dynasty that ruled Persia between 550 and 330 BCE.

acropolis fortified, elevated part of an ancient Greek city. The most famous such fortress is the Acropolis in Athens, Greece, where various large temples were built, including the Parthenon.

Ahura Mazda Zoroastrian god of light and truth.

Akhetaton city built by Akhenaton to replace the old Egyptian capital at Thebes; modern Amarna, Egypt.

Amarna Letters archive of clay tablets written in Babylonian cuneiform script; found at Akhetaton.

Amorites Semitic people who invaded Mesopotamia from the north and northwest around 2000 BCE. They were slowly absorbed into the Mesopotamian population.

Anatolia another name for Asia Minor (part of modern Turkey).

Aramaeans Semitic people who invaded southern Mesopotamia (Babylonia) around 1100 BCE. They slowly assumed the Babylonian culture and constituted a large part of the population.

archons magistrates in Athens, beginning around the seventh century BCE; elected annually. Their duties comprised legislation, the dispensation of justice, the conduct of religion, and military affairs. After the reforms of Cleisthenes, they were chosen by lot.

Assyrians people of northern Mesopotamia whose independent state, established in the 14th century BCE, became a major power in the region.

Astarte Canaanite and Phoenician goddess of procreation, fertility, and love. She was equated with the Semitic Ishtar and later associated with the Greek goddess Aphrodite. Astarte was also connected with Baal and was worshipped as the mother-goddess until Roman times.

Attica region of central Greece. Its chief city was Athens.

Babylon city in southern Mesopotamia that constituted a centralist Amorite empire under Hammurabi. Later, Babylon continued as the cultural and political capital of southern Mesopotamia. In 1595 BCE, the city was destroyed by the Hittites. From 612 to 539 BCE, Babylon was the capital of the Neo-Babylonian Empire.

Baghdad city built by Al-Mansur to appease the Persian Muslims; center of trade, industry, and Persian culture; destroyed by the Mongols.

Bosporus strait, 19 miles (30 km) long, that joins the Black Sea and the Sea of Marmara.

bronze copper-tin alloy widely used by 1700 BCE.

Bronze Age period during which bronze became the most important basic material; began around 3500 BCE in western Asia and around 1900 BCE in Europe.

Byblos first city in pre-Phoenician Levant to trade with Egypt. Around 1200 BCE, it was superseded as a trading center by Sidon and Tyre. Byblos was the center of the Astarte-Tammuz cult in Roman times.

Canaanites Semitic tribes who settled in Palestine and the western Levant in the third millennium BCE and mixed with the native population. They maintained separate city-states. Around 1200 BCE, their territory was infiltrated by Israelites and Philistines.

Carchemish Hittite trading city on the Euphrates River. After the fall of the Hittite Empire around 1200 BCE, it became the most important Neo-Hittite state. Carchemish was later conquered by the Assyrians.

Carthage city in northern Africa on the shores of the Mediterranean Sea; now a suburb of Tunis.

Corinth Greek town destroyed in 146 BCE for its resistance to Roman suppression. Rebuilt in 44 BCE as the capital of the Roman colony of Achaea on the orders of Julius Caesar.

cuneiform script consisting of characters pressed into clay with the use of styluses. It was used by the Sumerians and the Semites, though created by the native Mesopotamians. It started as images but evolved into a syllabic script.

Cycladic civilization Bronze Age civilization from around 3300 to 1000 BCE on the Greek Cyclades islands.

Damascus ancient capital of a city-state in Roman times; conquered variously by David of Israel, Assyrian Tiglath-pileser III in 732 BCE, and Alexander the Great in 333–332 BCE; part of the Seleucid kingdom until taken by Pompey the Great in 64 BCE. Made a Christian bishopric in the first century CE, it was taken over by Muslims in 635 CE and by Turks in 1056 CE. Damascus was besieged by the Christians in 1148 CE. In 1154 CE, it fell to the Egyptians. It was the headquarters of Saladin during the Third Crusade.

Dorians people from Macedonia and northern Greece who, armed with iron weapons, raided Egypt and neighboring areas in the 13th century BCE.

Euphrates river of western Asia that flows 1,740 miles (2,800 km) from eastern Turkey to the Persian Gulf.

Helladic culture Bronze Age culture from around 3300 to 1000 BCE on the Greek mainland.

hieroglyphs oldest Egyptian script. It was originally based on images, but later, as a result of the need to represent abstract concepts, it developed into a combination of ideograms, syllable signs, and letters.

Hittites people from Asia Minor who spoke an Indo-European language and settled in Asia Minor around 2000 BCE. They expanded their territory politically southward into Syria, Mesopotamia, and Canaan between 1650 and 1350 BCE. The Hittite Empire disappeared around 1200 BCE after the rise of Assyria and invasions by the Sea Peoples.

hoplites soldiers in the Greek heavy infantry, armed with swords, lances, and large round shields called hoplons.

Hurrians tribe from the east that settled in northern Mesopotamia around 1800 BCE. They founded the Mitanni Empire ruled by a militarily superior Indo-European elite. After 1200 BCE, the Hurrians settled in Urartu and from there conquered parts of Syria and Phoenicia.

Inanna Sumerian fertility goddess; daughter of Anu (the god of heaven and ruler of the gods). She merged with the Semitic god Ishtar during the Akkadian Empire and became the goddess of love and fertility.

Ionians Greek tribe driven from the mainland (except Attica) by the Dorians; settled on the Greek islands and on the west coast of Asia Minor in the ninth century BCE.

iron metallic element (chemical symbol Fe) that can be made into tools, weapons, and ornaments. It is extracted from iron ore by heating and hammering it for long periods. Iron was being processed in Anatolia, western Asia, by 3000 BCE. Iron is easier to work with than bronze.

Iron Age period during which major tools and weapons were made of iron; followed the Bronze Age. The Hittites formed the first Iron Age culture around 1700 BCE. Between 1200 and 600 BCE, ironworking spread over Asia and Europe.

Ishtar Semitic war goddess who merged with Inanna and became the goddess of love and fertility.

Israelites Semitic tribes who infiltrated Canaan in the second millennium BCE. They probably stayed in Egypt or in the border area between around 1650 and 1214 BCE. After 1200 BCE, they conquered Canaan, according to the Bible. They lived in a loose alliance of tribes but joined under a king around 1000 BCE.

Knossos Minoan settlement housing a large palace from the Second Palace period until around 1300 BCE.

Linear A script found on Minoan clay tablets in the palace complexes. Never deciphered, the script is probably a syllabic script and a simplified form of hieroglyphs.

Linear B script found on Mycenaean clay tablets on the Greek mainland and in Knossos. It is a syllabic script based on the characters of Linear A. The language of the Linear B tablets was not deciphered until 1953 CE.

Marathon city on the east coast of Attica where the Persians suffered a devastating defeat in 490 BCE by a small Athenian army under Miltiades.

Marduk Babylonian sun god. He became god of the state under Hammurabi and was considered the creator of Earth and god of wisdom.

Mari Semitic commercial center on the middle course of the Euphrates River. Its first flowering ended with the conquest by Sargon I, after which Mari was ruled by Akkad, Ur, and Ashur. Between around 1780 and 1760 BCE, Mari was again independent but was destroyed around 1760 BCE.

Medes nomadic horsemen who settled in Persia during the second millennium BCE. From around 700 BCE, they dominated a loose federation of tribes, including the Persians. Together with Babylon, they were responsible for the fall of the Assyrian Empire in 610 BCE.

Mesopotamia area in western Asia surrounding the Euphrates and Tigris rivers. (The word comes from the Greek meaning "between two rivers.") Floods and irrigation made the land fertile, and around 4500 BCE, the first agricultural settlements were founded there.

Messenia basin of the Pamisos River in the southwestern Peloponnese conquered by Sparta in the seventh century BCE.

Minoan civilization Bronze Age civilization on Crete from around 3300 to 1000 BCE, divided into the period before the palaces (3300–1900 BCE), the palace periods (1900–1200 BCE), and the period after the palaces (1200–1000 BCE).

Mycenae Bronze Age settlement on the Peloponnese where a palace fortress was built after 1450 BCE.

Heinrich Schliemann discovered Mycenae's rich royal tombs dating from the 16th century BCE.

Nile world's longest river at 4,132 miles (6,650 km). The river flows north from central Africa into Egypt, where in the final part of its course it forms a delta before reaching the Mediterranean Sea. During the annual rainy season in central Africa, the Nile River floods its banks, rendering the surrounding valley fertile and suitable for agriculture and horticulture.

Peloponnesian War (431–404 BCE) conflict of hegemony between Athens (generally allied with the Ionians) and Sparta (allied with the Dorians). The direct cause was a conflict about the island of Corcyra (modern Corfu). The army of Sparta annually destroyed Attica, while the Athenian fleet plundered the Peloponnesian coasts. Sparta finally triumphed over Athens with help from the Persians.

Persepolis important center of the Persian kingdom of the Achaemenids. From the reign of Darius, it was also a major royal citadel with multi-columned halls. Persepolis was destroyed by Alexander the Great.

Philistines Indo-European maritime people who settled in coastal Canaan at the end of the 13th century BCE. They drove the Israelites and the Canaanites out from the coastal area, forcing the Israelite tribes to organize centrally. King David of Israel and Judah ended their expansion.

Phoenicia mountainous country with a narrow coastal strip on the eastern Mediterranean Sea (modern Lebanon). Phoenicia was inhabited by local groups, mainly Canaanites. After Egyptian rule (c. 1500–1350 BCE) and Hittite rule (c. 1350–1200 BCE), it became independent around 1100 BCE. Phoenician forests were used for shipbuilding and timber export.

Poseidon Greek god of the sea, earthquakes, and volcanic phenomena; creator of the horse; brother of Zeus.

Sanskrit old Indo-Aryan language widely used in northern India as early as 1800 BCE.

Scythians herdsmen of Iranian stock who migrated from central Asia to southern Russia (principally the Crimea) in the eighth century BCE.

Sea Peoples groups who threatened the eastern Mediterranean coast, including the Nile Delta, during the time of the Ramesside kings of Egypt. The Philistines were one of the Sea Peoples.

Semites people residing in northern and southern Mesopotamia. They spoke a language different from the Sumerians and were largely rural dwellers. They founded the Akkadian Empire around 2335 BCE. The Akkadian and Sumerian civilizations rapidly became one.

Sidon city on the Phoenician coast that was a powerful trading center (c. 1400–700 BCE). Phoenicians were often called Sidonians.

Sparta city-state in the southern Peloponnese; isolated agricultural land power, resistant to external influences; oligarchy; fought Athens in the Peloponnesian War.

Sumerians people who settled in southern Mesopotamia (Sumer). They lived in independent city-states dominated by a temple economy. Lugalzaggisi tried to create a unified Sumerian state, but the rise of the Akkadian Empire around 2335 BCE prevented this.

Teshup Hurrian storm god who was adopted by the Hittites. He was the husband of the Hittite sun goddess Arinna and was considered the king of the heavens.

Thera volcanic island north of Crete where a Minoanlike civilization existed during the Bronze Age. A volcanic eruption destroyed Thera around 1500 BCE.

Thermopylae mountain pass between Thessaly and central Greece where Leonidas and hundreds of Spartans died covering the retreat of the Greek army from the Persians in 480 BCE.

Troy legendary city in Asia Minor near the entrance to the Dardanelles; besieged and destroyed by the Greeks during the Trojan War. Its ruins were discovered through the archaeological work of Heinrich Schliemann in the 19th century CE.

Tyre Phoenician city situated on an island off the coast of Lebanon. Tyre was a booming trade city from the 10th century BCE and founded many colonies, including Carthage.

Ugarit trading town in northern Canaan; Semitic city-state from the third millennium BCE. After reaching its height of power (c. 1550–1360 BCE), Ugarit was controlled by the Hittites. It was destroyed by the Sea Peoples around 1200 BCE.

Ur Sumerian city-state that constituted a centralized empire in Mesopotamia from around 2100 to 2000 BCE. Ur assumed a dominant position in the Lagash Empire. The Sumerian renaissance is called the Ur III period after the successful third dynasty in Ur.

Zoroastrianism traditional religion of Persians prior to conversion to Islam; founded by Zoroaster; posited competing spirits of good and evil.

MAJOR HISTORICAL FIGURES

Alexander the Great king of Macedonia; ruled between 336 and 323 BCE; son of Philip II; conquered the Persian Empire (334–330 BCE); conquered Syria and Egypt (333 BCE); invaded the Indus Valley (327 BCE).

Archilochus (c. 700 BCE) Greek poet and satirist from the island of Paros.

Cambyses II king of the Medes and Persians; ruled between 529 and 522 BCE; son of Cyrus the Great; conquered Egypt in 525 BCE.

Cyrus the Great king of the Persian Empire from 559 to 529 BCE and member of the Achaemenid dynasty. In 558 BCE, he obtained hegemony following an uprising against the Medes. He conquered Lydia in 547 BCE and the Neo-Babylonian kingdom around 539 BCE.

Darius I king of the Persian Empire between 521 and 486 BCE. He created political unity by dividing the empire into 20 satrapies, which were subject to central rule. He consolidated the borders, promoted trade, and developed an infrastructure. He was a follower of Zoroaster. He started the First Persian War, annexed Thrace and Macedonia, and undertook an expedition against Athens that ended in the Battle of Marathon.

David king of Israel and Judah between around 1000 and 965 BCE; successor to Saul. He defeated the Philistines, expanded the kingdom to its greatest size, seized Jerusalem from the Jebusites, and made it his capital.

Hammurabi king of Babylon from around 1792 to 1750 BCE; defeated the kings of Larsa and Assur and conquered Mari; drew up a legal code and abolished the deification of kings.

Hattusilis I king of the Old Hittite kingdom between around 1650 and 1620 BCE; founded Hattusas; tried to protect Hittite power against the Hurrians in Syria and the mountain peoples in Anatolia.

Herodotus (born c. 480 BCE) known as the father of Greek historiography. His work *History* viewed the centuries-long battle between the Greeks and the Persians as a confrontation between eastern and western cultures.

Hesiod (c. 700 BCE) Greek epic poet; author of *Thegony* (or *Birth of the Gods*), on religion and mythology, and *Works and Days*, a sort of manual for farmers.

Homer (c. 800 BCE) legendary Greek poet to whom the epics the *Iliad* and the *Odyssey* are attributed.

Leonidas (died 480 BCE) king of Sparta; killed at the Battle of Thermopylae with hundreds of Spartans covering the retreat of the main Greek army from the Persians.

Lycurgus ninth-century-BCE Spartan lawgiver and probable author of the Spartan constitution.

Merneptah king of Egypt from 1213 to 1203 BCE; successfully defended his country against a serious invasion from Libya.

Mursilis I Hittite king from around 1620 to 1590 BCE; conquered parts of Syria and razed Aleppo and Babylon.

Mursilis II Hittite king from around 1350 to 1320 BCE; resided in Hattusas; defended the Hittite Empire against surrounding states; conquered Asia Minor and fought the Egyptians.

Ramses II pharaoh of Egypt from 1279 to 1213 BCE. Among his numerous building projects were his own temple, the Ramesseum, and the expansion of the residence in Avaris.

Sargon II king of the Assyrians between 722 and 705 BCE; subjugated the Syrian and Phoenician coastal cities; defeated the Hurrians and the Aramaeans; became the king of Babylon.

Sennacherib king of the Assyrians between 704 and 681 BCE.

Solon sixth-century-BCE Athenian law reformer who abolished debt slavery in 594 BCE; expanded participation of all free citizens in government.

Suppiluliumas I Hittite king who ruled from around 1358 to 1323 BCE; expanded the Hittite Empire to its greatest size; conquered Syria with an organized army of charioteers; fought the Mitanni.

Tiglath-pileser III king of the Assyrians between around 746 and 727 BCE; conquered Babylon and was crowned its king.

Xerxes I king of Persia between 486 and 465 BCE; destroyed Athens in 480 BCE during the Second Persian War.

RESOURCES FOR FURTHER STUDY

BOOKS

Aubet, Maria Eugenia. *The Phoenicians and the West: Politics, Colonies, and Trade.* New York, 1993.

Baillie, M.G.L. *A Slice Through Time.* London, England, 1995.

Barber, Robin. *The Cyclades in the Bronze Age.* London, England, 1987.

Biers, William R. *The Archaeology of Greece: An Introduction.* Ithaca, NY, 1996.

Blegen, Carl W., and Marion Rawson. *A Guide to the Palace of Nestor.* Cincinnati, OH, 1962.

Boardman, John. *The Diffusion of Classical Art in Antiquity.* London, England, 1994.

———. *The Greeks Overseas: Their Early Colonies and Trade.* London, England, 1980.

Boardman, John (ed.). *The Oxford History of Classical Art.* New York, 1993.

Boardman, John, and David Finn. *The Parthenon and Its Sculptures.* London, England, 1985.

Bonfante, Larissa (ed.). *Etruscan Life and Afterlife.* Detroit, MI, 1986.

Brown, Shelby. *Late Carthaginian Child Sacrifice and Sacrificial Monuments in Their Mediterranean Context.* Sheffield, England, 1991.

Bryce, Trevor. *The Kingdom of the Hittites.* New York, 2005.

Burney, Charles, and David M. Lang. *The Peoples of the Hills: Ancient Ararat and Caucasus.* London, England, 1971.

Bury, J.B., and Russell Meiggs. *A History of Greece.* London, England, 1975.

Cadogan, Gerald. *Palaces of Minoan Crete.* London, England, 1976.

Cartledge, Paul. *The Spartans: The World of the Warrior-Heroes of Ancient Greece, from Utopia to Crisis and Collapse.* Woodstock, NY, 2003.

Chadwick, John. *The Decipherment of Linear B.* London, England, 1967.

———. *The Mycenaean World.* New York, 1976.

Cook, R.M. *Greek Painted Pottery.* London, England, 1972.

Coulton, J.J. *Greek Architects at Work.* Ithaca, NY, 1977.

Davis, Victor (ed.). *Hoplites: The Classical Greek Battle Experience.* New York, 1991.

Day, John. *Molech: A God of Human Sacrifice in the Old Testament.* New York, 1989.

Dickinson, Oliver. *The Aegean Bronze Age.* New York, 1994.

Dinsmoor, W.B. *The Architecture of Ancient Greece.* New York, 1975.

Doumas, Christos. *Thera: Pompeii of the Ancient Aegean.* London, England, 1983.

———. *The Wall-Paintings of Thera.* London, England, 1992.

Drews, Robert. *The End of the Bronze Age: Changes in Warfare and the Catastrophe ca. 1200 B.C.* Princeton, NJ, 1993.

Economakis, Richard (ed.). *Acropolis Restorations.* London, England, 1994.

Evans, Arthur. *The Palace of Minos at Knossos* (four volumes). Oxford, England, 1921–1935.

Forrest, W.G. *The Emergence of Greek Democracy.* London, England, 1966.

Forsyth, Phyllis Young. *Thera in the Bronze Age.* New York, 1997.

Getz-Preziosi, Patricia. *Sculptors of the Cyclades: Individual and Tradition in the Third Millennium B.C.* Ann Arbor, MI, 1987.

Green, Peter. *Alexander to Actium: The Hellenistic Age.* London, England, 1990.

Gurney, O.R. *The Hittites.* Baltimore, MD, 1952.

Herodotus (translated by George Rawlinson). *The Persian Wars*. New York, 1947.

Hesiod (translated by M.L. West). *Works & Days*. Oxford, England, 1978.

Homer (translated by Robert Fagles). *The Iliad*. New York, 1990.

———. *The Odyssey*. New York, 1996.

Hooker, J.T. *Reading the Past: Ancient Writing from Cuneiform to the Alphabet*. London, England, 1990.

Isager, Signe, and Jens Erik Skydsgaard. *Ancient Greek Agriculture: An Introduction*. London, England, 1992.

Jameson, Michael, Curtis Runnels, and Tjeerd van Andel. *A Greek Countryside: The Southern Argolid from Prehistory to the Present Day*. Stanford, CA, 1994.

Kriwaczek, Paul. *In Search of Zarathustra: The First Prophet and the Ideas that Changed the World*. New York, 2003.

Lancel, Serge. *Carthage: A History*. Oxford, England, 1995.

Lloyd, Seton. *The Archaeology of Mesopotamia*. London, England, 1978.

MacGillivray, J.A. *Sir Arthur Evans and the Archaeology of the Minoan Myth*. New York, 2000.

Macqueen, J.G. *The Hittites and Their Contemporaries in Asia Minor*. London, England, 1996.

Manning, Sturt. *Absolute Chronology of the Aegean Early Bronze Age*. Sheffield, England, 1995.

Moran, W.L. *The Amarna Letters*. Baltimore, MD, 1992.

Morris, Ian. *Burial and Ancient Society: The Rise of the Greek City-State*. New York, 1987.

Morris, Ian (ed.). *Classical Greece: Ancient Histories and Modern Archaeologies*. New York, 1994.

Moscati, Sabatino (ed.). *The Phoenicians*. Milan, Italy, 1988.

Mylonas, George E. *Mycenae and the Mycenaean Age*. Princeton, NJ, 1966.

Oates, Joan. *Babylon*. London, England, 1986.

Olmstead, A.T. *History of the Persian Empire: Achaemenid Period*. Chicago, IL, 1948.

Pallottino, Massimo. *The Etruscans*. Harmondsworth, England, 1978.

Pollitt, J.J. *Art and Experience in Classical Greece*. Cambridge, England, 1972.

Rasmussen, Tom, and Nigel Spivey (eds.). *Looking at Greek Vases*. New York, 1991.

Renfrew, Colin. *The Cycladic Spirit*. London, England, 1991.

———. *The Emergence of Civilization: The Cyclades and the Aegean in the Third Millennium B.C.* London, England, 1972.

Rhodes, Robin F. *Architecture and Meaning on the Athenian Acropolis*. New York, 1995.

Ridgway, David. *The First Western Greeks*. New York, 1992.

Roaf, Michael. *Cultural Atlas of Mesopotamia and the Ancient Near East*. New York, 1990.

Robertson, Martin. *The Art of Vase-Painting in Classical Athens*. New York, 1992.

Russell, John Malcolm. *Sennacherib's Palace without Rival at Nineveh*. Chicago, IL, 1991.

Sandars, Nancy K. *The Sea Peoples*. London, England, 1985.

Scarre, Chris, and Rebecca Stefoff. *The Palace of Minos at Knossos*. New York, 2003.

Schlitz, Laura Amy. *The Hero Schliemann*. Cambridge, MA, 2006.

Sekunda, Nick. *Marathon 490 BC: The First Persian Invasion of Greece*. Westport, CT, 2005.

Shanks, Michael. *Art and the Early Greek State: An Interpretive Archaeology*. New York, 1999.

Soren, David, Aicha Ben Abed Khader, and Hedi Slim. *Carthage: Uncovering the Mysteries and Splendors of Ancient Tunisia*. New York, 1990.

Spivey, Nigel, and Simon Stoddart. *Etruscan Italy: An Archaeological History*. London, England, 1990.

Taylour, William. *The Mycenaeans*. New York, 1983.

Wace, Alan. *Mycenae: An Archaeological History and Guide.* Princeton, NJ, 1949.

Walker, C.B.F. *Cuneiform*. Berkeley, CA, 1987.

Warren, Peter. *The Aegean Civilizations*. Oxford, England, 1989.

Warren, Peter, and Vronwy Hankey (eds.). *Aegean Bronze Age Chronology*. Bristol, England, 1989.

Whitelaw, K.W., and R.B. Coote. *The Emergence of Israel in Historical Perspective.* Sheffield, England, 1987.

Wiseman, D. J. *Nebuchadnezzar and Babylon*. New York, 1985.

Woods, Michael. *In Search of the Trojan War*. Berkeley, CA, 1985.

Wycherley, R.E. *The Stones of Athens.* Princeton, NJ, 1978.

Yoffee, Norman. *The Economic Role of the Crown in the Old Babylonian Period.* Malibu, CA, 1977.

WEB SITES

Cuneiform
Interactive Web site about cuneiform writing
http://www.upennmuseum.com/cuneiform.cgi

Greek Dialects
Guide to the major linguistic variants of the Greek language; includes a family tree
http://www.columbia.edu/~rcc20/greece3.html

Hesiod
Facts about the life of the ancient Greek poet; includes links to translations of his work
http://ancienthistory.about.com/cs/people/p/hesiod.htm

Hittites
History of the ancient Anatolian civilization; complete with maps
http://www.crystalinks.com/hittites.html

Hittites (International World History Project)
History of the Hittites; discusses their cities, kings, art, and contributions to civilization
http://history-world.org/hittites.htm

Homer
Introduction to the poet's work; includes background information
http://www.wsu.edu/~dee/MINOA/HOMER.HTM

Hoplites
Detailed description of the hoplites' equipment and function in battle
http://digilander.libero.it/tepec/the_athenian_hoplite.htm

Knossos
Detailed guide to the palace on the Greek island of Crete
http://www.interkriti.org/visits/knosos.htm

Lycurgus
Account of the life of the Spartan statesman
http://www.e-classics.com/lycurgus.htm

Minoan Writing
Essay about the Linear B writing system
http://www.omniglot.com/writing/linearb.htm

Mycenaeans
History of the Mycenaean culture
http://www.historywiz.com/mycenaean-mm.htm

Persepolis
Illustrated guide to the ancient Persian city
http://www.persia.org/imagemap/perspolis.html

Persian Wars
General overview of the conflict; includes links to more specialized material
http://www.socialstudiesforkids.com/subjects/persianwars.htm

INDEX